Organizing and Directing
CHILDREN'S CHOIRS

Organizing and Directing
Children's Choirs

MADELINE D. INGRAM

♪
ABINGDON PRESS
NEW YORK • NASHVILLE

ORGANIZING AND DIRECTING CHILDREN'S CHOIRS

Copyright © MCMLIX by Abingdon Press

The Library of Congress has
cataloged this book as follows:

Ingram, Madeline D. Organizing and directing
children's choirs. New York, Abingdon Press
[1959]. 160 p. 20 cm. 1. Choirs (Music)
2. Conducting, Choral. I. Title. MT88.I5
784.96   59—8197 ‡

B

SET UP, PRINTED, AND BOUND BY THE
PARTHENON PRESS, AT NASHVILLE,
TENNESSEE, UNITED STATES OF AMERICA

Foreword

EVERY CHOIR DIRECTOR FROM THE PROFESSIONAL to the amateur has experienced a sinking feeling as he faced a children's choir program for the first time. Even though he may have had extensive training and experience with adult choirs he is faced with problems that were not discussed in the classroom. For the phenomenal growth of children's choirs and the multiple choir program has caught many schools of music without any course to offer or guidance to give to students.

One school which has led the way is Lynchburg College in Lynchburg, Virginia, where for several years a course in children's choir work has been taught by Madeline Ingram—head of the department of music as well as Minister of Music at Memorial Methodist Church in Lynchburg. Several church leaders have suggested that Mrs. Ingram write a book, but she has declined on the grounds that she did not have the time and did not like to write. Finally she agreed to record the classroom lectures on tape, and the present book is based on those tapes.

No attempt has been made to eliminate the personal touches and references, for this book is not a philosophy of the children's choir (although one senses a profound underlying philosophy), but is rather a guide to the young choir director, showing how Mrs. Ingram works with the multiple choir program in her church. Therefore the suggestions made are practical and have been proved in week to week rehearsals and services.

Mrs. Ingram's services as a lecturer and choir festival director have taken her to all parts of the country, and literally thousands of singers and directors have felt the impact of her warm personality and sound words of advice. The reader will sense this warmth and at the same time will find a common sense approach to choir work which will guide him to the solution of many problems.

It has been a joy to work with Mrs. Ingram in the preparation of this material, and it is our joint hope that this book will serve the needs of many choir directors.

AUSTIN C. LOVELACE

Contents

Why Children's Choirs?

CHAPTER I

CHILDREN'S CHOIRS! WHAT WONDERFUL PICTURES those words bring to mind! Row upon row of vested children marching in processional up the church aisle happily singing "Joyful, Joyful, We Adore Thee"; or a group of shiny-eyed choristers singing Christmas carols while the candlelight dances merrily over their eager faces; or a dignified choir of worshiping children occupying the choir stalls usually filled by the older choir and lending the beauty of their young voices to anthems, hymns, and responses. And what patterns of Christian devotion and discipline are set for others by these youthful servants of the church.

Many church musicians think of children's choirs as phenomena of the past ten or twenty years, but the movement actually started over sixty years ago in the First Presbyterian Church at Flemington, New Jersey. Elizabeth Van Fleet Vosseller, the founder, felt that the children of her church and community needed more music in their religious education than they were receiving in their Sunday school experience, so she started with a choir of four girls from the church. The history of this beginning is found in her book *The Use of a Children's Choir in the Church.*

The program which Miss Vosseller began was experimental. There were few guideposts along the way, and trial and error was the method of procedure. Since there were no standards, she set her own. The standards and procedures of that early day are not always followed now, but Miss Vosseller's basic educational principles still hold good today and should be studied by all who would be successful directors. While many fine leaders have visited the choir school in Flemington, have studied the program with care, and have used many of the ideas of those early days, in general most directors faced with the task of developing a youth choir program have cleared their own paths in the wilderness with little or no guidance.

Today there is still no specific children's choir method. Some churches have developed elaborate programs, including choirs for all ages from the tiny tots to the young people of high school and college age. In other churches there are only one or two choirs with age groupings in various patterns. Schools of sacred music offer some few courses but most help comes from suggestions by friends and colleagues who are willing to share the results of what has succeeded in their churches. One source of ideas is the monthly mimeographed paper of The Choristers Guild, 47 El Arco Drive, Santa Barbara, California. More and more church periodicals and music magazines are carrying helpful articles written by leading church musicians.

As the choir movement has expanded directors have found themselves faced with problems. A basic question is, "What ages should be put together?" For many years all children's choirs were called junior choirs, and included any age below the adult level. Sometimes the age span ranged from six or seven to fifteen and sixteen. Today we realize the absurdity of applying the same educational principles to these extremes in age.

Another question bothers many directors, "What shall we do with the choir?" Often the thoughts seem to be: "We have a junior choir. Isn't it wonderful? Aren't they sweet? Don't they look pretty? Don't they sing like little angels? We must put them on show in church some Sunday—it will draw a big crowd." The result is a performance. Often it is a case of the choir's parading to the front of the sanctuary or to some conspicuous spot where they perform. Considerable attention is called to the fact that here is a "special" choir, and consequently worship suffers. Both parents and children must be taught to take all choir music out of the category of special performances.

These two questions alone indicate in a small way the need for careful thought and planning before a children's choir program is undertaken in any church. Let us assume that you are trying to convince your church that choirs should be started. The music committee would want to know why they are necessary. What advantages are there in having children's choirs?

Consider the advantages to the church. First of all, the choir program helps to develop leadership. The Episcopal Church has drawn heavily on former choir boys for its rectors, and many a

13

boy with a good voice has been attracted from another denomination because of the choir. Likewise many a child has been drawn to church membership through a choir program. As a child learns to love and serve the church through the choir he is developing leadership ability which will help guide the church of tomorrow. Many people who should be the leaders in some field of church activity feel an inadequacy because they were never prepared in any way to be leaders. Leadership does not necessarily evolve from mere church attendance; it is more apt to come from active participation in service of the church. With the population of the United States growing rapidly, and many church-school walls bulging at the seams, the church has opportunity and responsibility to develop leadership for the future.

A second advantage to the church lies in stimulating and holding the interest of the child, thus producing a loyalty and concern when he is older. All children love to sing and often sing little tunes before they begin to talk. These are spontaneous outbursts which should be encouraged and developed. That the free, selfless expression of joy is often stifled along the way, the mute, self-conscious adult is sad evidence. The children's choir program can be a means of encouraging and developing the God-given instinct for song. The child will be interested and happy in his church and will be loyal to it in years to come.

It is a sad commentary that the church has failed to keep pace with the music program of many public schools, where music that is interesting and challenging is offered for participation. And now with the advent of radio, television, and hi-fi recordings, our children have opportunities to hear fine music well performed. These media recognize the fact that children like music, and all too often our children are taught finer church music by better methods outside the church than within it.

14

Another advantage to the church is the beauty and dignity that a well-trained children's choir can contribute to the worship service. There is a kind of ethereal, impersonal quality in a child's voice which is suited to church music. If the voice is properly trained and protected, it has none of the problems of the adult soprano voice. Children are not as susceptible to emotional difficulties which cause so many vocal problems in adults, so the contribution can be a vital and beautiful one to the church.

A fourth advantage is the child's regular attendance Sunday after Sunday, and most important, his intelligent participation in the worship service. One of the director's biggest jobs is that of training in worship. The church-school experiences are often only training periods for worship and are different from the regular morning service of worship in church. Sharing in this service helps children grow in their appreciation of the worship experience, but at the same time participation in it calls for careful preparation and planning and places a special responsibility on the children.

The choir helps teach the mechanics of the service. We see the necessity for thought and planning if a service is to be worshipful. It cannot be thrown together at the last moment. Any fine service is planned with logical reasons for each movement, yet many people are not conscious of this because they have had no opportunity to learn it. Training for worship makes worship more meaningful and enjoyable, and joyous participation leads others to participate. Children with choir experience become adept in following the order of worship, finding responsive readings, and standing promptly for the singing of hymns. Part of this is habit, but the habit develops from understanding the necessity of being prepared. Such leadership is a leavening agent in any congregation. Truly, "a little child shall lead them."

A growing church membership is another advantage to the

15

church. Early loyalty, developed in the children's choir, often leads to church membership. More evangelism takes place in the choirs than we realize, for the choir director can make an impact on the lives of children as great as that of the minister. He has more time with the children, knows them more intimately, and works with them musically year after year. Over a span of time the impact of great music devotedly sung for the church as a part of a singing fellowship can lead to intelligent and devoted church membership.

When you reach the child you will often reach the families. A good choir program attracts many people to a church, and a child who thinks the choir program is fine invites his friends. In growing metropolitan areas the community church is cutting across denominational lines, and the church nearby is the easiest to attend. The parents will be inclined to attend where the children feel most at home. The choir program can be a strong point in reaching and holding new people.

The choir program through annual projects helps to educate the parents. For example, one year a particular study project may be the Christian year. Many people do not know much about this subject. Advent is perhaps occasionally mentioned; Christmas of course is celebrated; Lent is mentioned, but little is done about it; Holy Week is something vague; Palm Sunday receives some attention; and at Easter everyone comes to church for the second time during the year. Some never hear of other seasons such as Pentecost and Trinity Sunday. Yet there is an advantage in knowing something about the seasons of the year and their deeper meanings.

In our church, with the choir studying the Christian year, the parents were soon asking pertinent questions about what the children were studying. The choir director was invited to spend half an hour each Sunday for six weeks in the Adult Fellowship class to enable the parents to study the Christian year also. When the choir studied symbols and their use in church, the adults wanted to be taught. Another project was built around the hymnal, and again an opportunity was afforded to teach the parents. Thus the choir project became an educational program for the entire church.

The choir program also strengthens the link between church school and the church—a link which is sometimes weak. There is often a big gap between the two, for each is inclined to go its own way. Church school does not replace the service of worship, but is a training ground for every individual of the church. The children's choirs, which are drawn from the members of the church school, are the connecting link which inspires a feeling of unity in the total program.

Let us turn next to what the choir program can do for the individual. Belonging to a choir gives deeper meaning to a child's membership in the church. Most churches are alert to the fact that the youth must be reached and brought into the fold of the church. Classes for membership are held and eventually the children find their names on the church roll. Then what happens? Nothing. The children find themselves squeezed out of the fellowship in the morning worship service because the service is usually entirely designed for adults. It is little wonder that our youth drop out of the church at junior high and high school age. But if a child has come through a fine choir program and has participated in the morning worship service on a regular basis he has a sense of belonging which ties him to the church, making church membership more meaningful.

Some children get most of their musical education in a choir program. The church, through the choir, offers musical training as an inducement and the training will have real value to the individual. The church has always been an educative force, though not always an educative force in music.

If a choir program is good it will not only be educating in singing, which is vitally important, but it will also be educating in various other allied arts, plus various fields of music. There should be music to hear which might not be heard otherwise. Children can gain a great deal by listening to what the adult choir sings. The choir learns to adapt to many situations through singing in various locations in the sanctuary, singing with different voice combinations, and singing with various instruments.

There is a certain give and take which is a valuable lesson for living. There is the realm of personal relations, for every children's choir should be open to every child who wants to sing. The choir is truly a democratic group—not a selective one. Therefore individual responsibility is very important. Each member must learn to respond to the unity of the group and must co-operate to a high degree. He cannot shirk his share of the load. Over the years we help to build Christian character through the choir experience.

The choir also offers social contacts which are helpful in developing a well-rounded personality. Friendships are formed. Good times are had at parties.

With so much to offer to the church and to the child, the choir program needs no apology. The real question is, "How can a church afford not to have a choir program?"

The Choir Director

CHAPTER **II**

Before starting a choir program we should find out what is required of a director, for the program rises or falls at the point of leadership. If a choir program fails, the reason may be that the leadership is indifferent. It probably was not at first, for the director may be fired with enthusiasm when he begins. But as time goes by and rehearsal follows rehearsal with dreadful regularity and insistency, the fire dies and the director gets careless. Inspiration is lacking and the slump begins. As the director slumps so does the choir, and a vicious circle develops. Sometimes it is not lack of interest but lack of adequate knowledge. Left to his own initiative and experience he finds that it is hard to keep the choir rehearsals interesting.

It has been argued that only women can direct children's choirs successfully, since their voices are of the same pitch level and quality as children's. Yet some of the most successful directors are men. Male directors should sing lightly, but in their own range and children are easily able to repeat the tones in their own octave. Demonstration of good soprano tone can be made by a soprano from the high school or adult choir. Some directors also use flute or violin as tone patterns. So we can think in terms of people of both sexes working ably with children's voices.

Perhaps the most important characteristic of a fine director is the ability to think creatively and imaginatively. You can read articles in magazines, study books, attend workshops, and take advantage of all materials, but unless you have the fresh outlook of a child you will have a hard time winning children's attention and co-operation.

Even more important possibly than musical skill is a love of children. If you do not love children, do not consider working with them. Many people find it difficult to gear themselves to a child's attitude or to think as a child. They either talk down to him as if he were a baby, or they treat him as an adult. Either extreme is poor and can cause the child to lose his interest in the choir and his devotion to the director. Each child is an individual, a human being, a personality in a particular stage of development which never stands still.

The director must know what can be expected of a primary, a junior, or an adolescent. He must learn to recognize the signs of the levels of development in personality. He should learn the physical characteristics, particularly the different rates of development between boys and girls in adolescence. Both boys and girls have a change of voice, and the director has to know how to give help through this difficult time. He needs to know what can be expected of the voice—how far it can go. He must remember that the voice of a child cannot be constantly pushed without ruining it for life. The little child's voice has a high, light, floating quality which must be protected and cultivated.

Personality problems must also be met with sympathy and knowledge. The adolescent child, for example, is very difficult to understand because he does not understand himself. He is neither an adult nor a child; some days he is one and some days he is the other. One day he co-operates and moves at an adult level; the next he seems impossible. Physically he is slow, as are his reactions. The director must be sympathetic to his problems and needs and have a sincere desire to help. The love and understanding of children, then, is of prime importance.

Creative planning is also a necessity. I once heard a Sunday-school superintendent come into a class of adult women and say "I need a teacher for the young children's class. The regular teacher sent word she wouldn't be here and I want a volunteer to teach them today." When nobody volunteered, he called a woman by name and said, "Can't you go?" When she protested that she was not prepared and did not know what the children were studying, he remarked, "You don't have to be prepared to work with children; you just go and talk to them for awhile. That is all that is necessary."

Unfortunately, many people have this misconception. A director will find that he needs to do his hardest and finest work with children. The children's choir presents a new field—one of challenge and promise. The director must be prepared to meet his responsibilities of choir leadership.

It takes an attractive personality to work with children, for they respond quickly and easily to a happy, cheerful person. Children are essentially happy and cheerful themselves, and they do not enjoy being with a person who is gloomy, or whose face is always tinged with sadness.

The director needs a sense of humor. You need the ability to laugh with children at things which, by your standards, are not funny, but which they want to share with you. You will find yourself laughing time after time when the children are "in stitches" and you have not the slightest notion of what is funny. You will be bombarded annually with the same jokes and riddles. (Of course you never heard the answers!) Above all you need to be able to laugh at yourself when you make a mistake.

Another characteristic of an attractive personality is enthusiasm. If your enthusiasm is contagious and infectious, as it should be, the children will be carried along in the program by the current of your obvious interest.

Add to this, imagination, for children live in a realm of imagination. They go through the stage of having imaginary playmates and imaginary pets to whom they talk, and they expect you to know all about them too. If you wish to test this quality of imagination, make up a story about a squirrel, a rabbit, or even a bettle—let your imagination run wild and see the wide-eyed expectancy on the part of the children as they wonder what will happen next. An interesting chapter on this subject of imagination is found in Davison's *Church Music—Illusion and Reality*.

Since your voice is such an important tool it may be well to ask yourself these questions concerning it. Is it pleasing? High pitched? Muffled? Nasal? Your speaking voice is almost more important than your singing voice. Let me cite an example. In a junior choir festival rehearsal several years ago there was a director who had a marvelous way with children. They all loved her instantly. She did not raise her voice, but spoke slowly and clearly enough for them to understand every word. Her voice commanded attention and the children listened because her voice reflected her warmth and love. During the entire rehearsal the children were attentive. Then another director got up to make announcements and immediately the children became restless, began talking to each other, and paid no attention to the announcements. Why? The second director had raised her voice, which was loud and nasal, and she lost the children. She had a tone of demanding and scolding in her voice. The first director had a quality which commanded attention through quietness.

Voices are important. They can create quietness or restlessness. There are voices that are pleasing; there are voices that are annoying. We instinctively judge people as we listen to them speak—their character shines through. Since you will spend a great deal of time in talking with children it is necessary to work at your speech. Most rehearsals will come at a time of day when your voice will not be at its best. As the day wears on you will tend to wear out vocally. It is easy for the strain of the day to show, so learn to control your voice so that it sounds alert and alive.

The ability to organize efficiently is also necessary for good leadership. A disorganized approach cannot succeed, but an orderly approach, putting things in sequence and importance, will carry a director through a difficult rehearsal.

Initiative is inherent in good leadership. There will be many battles to be fought, problems to be overcome, requests for funds to be made—and the director must take the lead in these matters.

And patience! It takes a world of patience to work with people.

Whether you work with small children or older people you need to be patient. It takes months, even years, to build a fine program, and you must not be impatient if the choir does not sound perfect after one rehearsal or one month or one year of rehearsals. There will be misunderstandings and disagreements, but patience will help overcome these.

A good personal check list is found in *So to Speak* by Elizabeth von Hesse. If you are not the sparkling personality you thought you were, do not be discouraged. It used to be thought that a person either received a good personality when such things were passed around or else he was behind the door at the time. But personality can be developed. Since you are to be an example before children work on yourself first. All people respond to a pleasing personality and children will make an immediate response to your personality— for good or for ill.

One particular quality which a director needs is firmness. Children do not really want to get away with murder, as is so often said, but they will try you out to the limit. They want to know whether you mean what you say, and they will respect you if you are firm. They have no respect for the person who does not require the finest from them. The business of facing children with firmness and love is important, and once a working relationship is established you must constantly strive to keep it alive. This involves making rules which are both fair and workable. Life is made easier for all when the choir members know what is expected of them. Over the years the observance of the rules will lead to the establishment of desirable habits.

Some directors hesitate to make rules and regulations and instead rely on the hail-fellow-well-met approach, particularly with older children of high-school age. There is a real danger here. It is undoubtedly helpful for the director to be able to go swimming or play baseball with his choir and be one of the group, and yet there must be a point at which there is a difference in status. Under no circumstances should you allow the children to call you by your first name. This delicate balance of difference is often hard to find, but it must be understood from the beginning. If the director makes the mistake of being unapproachable on his high pedestal of superiority, he loses the choir. But if he makes the mistake of being too familiar, he also runs the risk of losing the respect of the choir.

A choir director must be a child psychologist. If you have had no courses on child psychology there is no need for worry. There are many fine books in libraries that will help. Several are listed in the Bibliography. Helpful magazine articles about children appear frequently, and the good director is a lifetime student of the techniques of understanding children.

Directors are also educators, for ours is a teaching job. We must know how to teach and what methods are best. If the children do not like the choir, or if the parents lose their interest, the fault in most cases lies with the director and his inadequate teaching methods. The whole attitude of the director is most important at this point, for children follow his lead, absorbing the kind of music he teaches. Therefore what you teach and how you teach are most important. If you feel inadequate because of lack of training, look around for opportunities; the public school music teachers are working with the same children you will teach, and their methods of music teaching have constantly been improving. There are educators' magazines which will be of help. And of course there are adult night classes in various fields of education and psychology which can improve your methods of teaching.

Not only are we teachers of music, but we must be teachers of religion also. The choir director should be a religious guide to the children, so he must constantly be growing spiritually. This involves a dedication of self to the high calling of the church and commitment to growth in the area of religion. Every rehearsal, every anthem, every hymn, offers an opportunity to help children grow spiritually if the right emphasis is made.

We must be students—students of everything. The church-school literature must be studied so there is correlation of effort and materials. There must be study of religion, study of music, study of methods, the arts, vocal methods, and anything which helps to make a well-rounded individual. Children will only respect you when they feel that you are an authority—that you know what you are saying. If you do not have a solid basis of knowledge and try to get by with subterfuge the children will see through you quickly, for children are not easily fooled. They are masters at analyzing people. It is easy to try to bulldoze your way through tight spots, but the choir program and the children will suffer. So study to show thyself an approved workman.

Starting a Children's Choir Program

CHAPTER **III**

 WE HAVE BEEN TALKING ABOUT OURSELVES AND the importance of our work, but it is time now to organize the choir program. Unless you plan carefully the program can easily fail. It is not enough to want a program; you must spend time and effort getting your entire church enthusiastic about it. Perhaps you are enthusiastic to the bursting point, but does the rest of the church share your enthusiasm? It takes time to get everybody interested, informed, and moving with you; so you must make plans to talk with a number of people.

For the moment let us assume that you do not know whether anybody but you in your church is interested in starting a children's choir, for perhaps the idea is entirely your own. First you want to go to the minister. If he is not interested, the program cannot succeed. You must point out the values to the church and to the children, and he must come to share your enthusiasm. You should discuss plans, objectives, procedures for starting, how the choir will be used, when it will sing, and anything else which relates the choir to the total program of the church.

You must also present the program to the music committee so they can make recommendations to the official bodies of the church. They will ask you to outline the entire program and to indicate the costs involved. They will want to know if you expect to buy vestments, how many you will need, and what the cost will be. The costs for music and other materials should also be prepared for their study and question. Mere approval is not enough—the music committee must also catch your enthusiasm and be willing to stand behind the program wholeheartedly.

It is the duty of the music committee to make recommendations to the board of the church concerning the program that you have outlined, and you will probably be asked to appear before this group. It will probably be a solemn-faced group who must pronounce careful judgment upon your request. What is the cost will be a thought uppermost in their minds. You need to be able to give estimates of the cost but you need even more to present the spiritual values inherent in a choir program. Be prepared to answer any and all questions openly and honestly. To do this calls for much thought and planning. Think through everything that could be asked and what your answers would be.

While all this is taking place through the official channels of the church you should be talking with other people. One is the director of Christian education if there is such a person on the staff. There will be scheduling problems to consider—when the children will rehearse and when they will sing. There may be conflicts in time and interest if you do not talk these matters through in advance. You should ask for information about suggested music in the lesson units, special services for which the choir could sing, and basic viewpoints and objectives of the educational program. Show that you wish to make the choir experience a continuation of the religious education of the children rather than a program competing for time and interest. In our church the director of Christian education makes use of the choir afternoon for an extended church-school session, sitting down with the children before rehearsal and laying foundations for work which will be done musically later in the choir rehearsal.

Another person of great importance is the church-school superintendent. He knows the families and children almost better than anyone else. He knows who can be counted on for co-operation and can advise you as to leaders for the Mother's Guild program. He can encourage the children to join the choirs, and he certainly should share in the planning.

At this point you are ready to talk to the parents of the children. If possible visit in the homes so you come to know the home environment and the relations between parents and children. It helps to see the children in the home—to see how they react in a familiar environment. If you cannot visit in all of the homes because of the pressures of time and schedule you can still meet the parents in the church-school classes, in the Mr. and Mrs. Club, or in some other scheduled meeting which the parents attend. The Sunday morning class is perhaps the best time, but you should make arrangements with the officers in advance so they know you are coming and can give you adequate time for a presentation. Be brief and to the point—give as clear a picture as possible of your plans and what you expect of the parents and children. It is perhaps wise to make your visit to such a class an annual affair, for you will reach people then who may be missed in your first recruitment of choir members.

There are, of course, other meetings where an announcement will be helpful, such as an informal gathering during the week, a women's group meeting, or a family night supper. Wherever you present your program make clear to the parents that you expect a choir member to be regular—that only excused absences are permitted, and that a good excuse is illness or death in the family. Let the parents know that it is their responsibility to see that the children attend regularly and that events are not scheduled which will interfere with the choir program. This perhaps sounds as if it will scare people away from the program, but a choir cannot be built on any other foundation.

Finally, you want to reach the children themselves. Too often a choir director beginning a program starts here, but that is a mistake. If you are enthusiastic and have made all the other leaders enthusiastic you will have children responding and bringing their friends. You will have already met most of the children in the homes. The aggressive ones who may be disciplinary problems are already known to you, and you will plan how to deal with them. The timid children will get a kind extra word of encouragement. You will have observed the children in their various classes in church school, and you will have some idea of the group leaders. Almost any teacher will be happy to give you a few minutes of time in each class, and a visit will arouse the interest you want. It is of particular importance that you observe the leaders among the children as you make your visits—the aggressive ones whom the others imitate. If you get the leaders in the choir, the rest will follow. If the leaders decide they do not like the choir, you have a hard time ahead in getting the others interested.

All this preliminary contact with the children should take place in September. Of course you will set the dates for your rehearsals and ask the parents to keep them clear in the calendar, but for the first year it is perhaps best to let the children get started in their school activities, music lessons, and other programs so that not too much new material is presented at the beginning of the school year. However, after the first season the program should begin with school, or maybe even before so that the choir program has a chance to get a head start on other activities and before the children become so heavily scheduled that they cannot add anything more to their programs.

In the meantime you should get out publicity—articles in the church bulletin and in the public newspapers. The church bulletin should carry a brief article each week, attractively worded and to the point. Whet the curiosity of the children so they want to come to see what is happening. Many churches mimeograph or print a very attractive brochure describing the various choirs, age groupings, purposes of the choirs, attendance rules, rehearsal times, and some of the programs to be presented during the year. These can be inexpensively prepared. Of course there should be posters advertising the choir program placed in the halls of the church and in the classrooms.

If you do not play the piano yourself, you must secure a good accompanist for the choir. Even if you do play it is advantageous to have an accompanist. The church organist or pianist may be the logical person if she has the time to give to the rehearsals. If not, consult her for suggestions and perhaps set a time for auditions

31

for prospects. It is wise to check the accompanying ability of a pianist, for many fine pianists play concert pieces brilliantly but cannot sight-read a simple hymn tune. A pianist who can also sing will be an asset, for such a person "feels" with the singing better than a nonsinger.

If you will need other helpers in the choir program, secure these before the season starts. List all of your needs, and then find the people to assist you.

Choir Organization

IV

How SHOULD THE CHILDREN BE DIVIDED INTO choirs? What age groupings are best? These are questions which every director must face. A closely graded choir program is fine provided there is a sufficient number of children in each age group to form an adequate choir. Such a system takes the child through a series of choirs with a graded course of study in church music and should follow closely the pattern of the graded church school.

The starting age depends upon many factors—first, how much

33

time you can give for the choir program (a full-time minister of music is desirable for every church that can support one). If your time is limited, you will have to decide where it is most important to start. If there can only be one graded choir, probably the best group would be a junior age group of nine-, ten-, and eleven-year-olds. This does leave a blank spot between the juniors and adults, but the junior age group has more enthusiasm than any other in the church and that enthusiasm will help to create interest in choir work in general.

Primary age choirs of six-, seven-, and eight-year-old children are functioning well in many situations. Such choirs are largely training groups rather than participating groups in regular worship services. Bringing a choir of these children into a Sunday service causes a distraction to the worshiper and adds nothing of significance to the worship experience of the child. They may be used in less formal situations such as a Christmas carol sing, but it is to be hoped that their public appearances are very, very few.

Although the primary age is that of six-, seven-, and eight-year-olds, there is a wide disparity of skills and abilities between the six- and the eight-year-old. The eight-year-old can read; he is started in school work and can do things more quickly than the younger children. He is still very young in many ways, but he resents the slowness of the smaller children in the choir. So instead of grouping six-, seven-, and eight-year-olds it is perhaps better to form a second choir of only the seven- and eight-year-olds since they are fairly close in development and to bring the five-year-old into the group of six-year-olds.

At the junior age there is the question of whether to separate boys and girls. Some directors do not and have no trouble combining the two. Others find that the boys do better by themselves and that more boys are drawn to the program if they feel they have a choir of their own. There is also involved the question of the boy's changing voice, and the boys' choir probably would include boys from the age of nine until voice change—a span which is larger than the junior age grouping. So it perhaps is wise to divide for this reason if there is an adequate number of boys for separate choirs. The divided choirs also make it possible to use two different approaches—for what appeals to junior girls often does not appeal to the boys. When they are combined the boys have a tendency to be silly and to quarrel with the girls—because they are conscious of each other and do not know how to act when together. The director has to make his own decision as to whether to divide or not. Usually both groups would learn much of the same music and would sing together in the church services.

The choirs above the junior age would best be grouped according to the church-school division. Intermediate age girls usually work best alone as a choir since most boys are then having trouble with voice change. However, there are successful choirs which include boys and girls of this age. The high-school age choir of course will include both sexes, and the more boys the better for the choir. Some school systems use the two and four grouping for junior high and high school, and others use the three and three. Where this does not parallel the church division one must use his own best judgment as to which grouping fits best into the choir program. It often seems best to have the high-school group together for four years if possible since it gives enough time for the boys' voices to settle sufficiently to be of maximum help in the choir.

In the small church where it is not possible to have graded choirs because of the small number of children, a choir may well be made up of children of a wider age span. Nine-year-olds can work well with boys and girls of junior-high age, but younger children will become quickly discouraged and disinterested if they are expected to work as rapidly as these older singers. This grouping of nine- to fourteen-year-olds is far from ideal, but in a small church there is a closer knit feeling which can overcome age differences. If the director understands the problems involved and gives the personal attention to each child that is necessary in any choir program the children can work together well. It would then be best to let the high-school age join with the adults, after you have discussed with each the problems involved in such an arrangement.

In the fall many choirs have a pre-registration period during which time all children are notified by card of rehearsal dates and times. The card is returned to the church indicating the desire to join the choir for the season, giving name, address, telephone, and name of choir member. During the rest of the year the director must keep up with newcomers through contacts with the choir children and their parents (when a new child moves into the neighborhood) and through the church office as new persons join.

On registration day helpers will be needed to take care of the children. If the choir members are too young to write, someone must fill out the registration cards. It is perhaps best for the director to do this, for it gives an opportunity to talk to the child and to get the name and face fixed together. The same type of card can be used for all children, with the cards sorted according to choirs. Of if you wish you can use a different colored card for each choir, but the same basic information should be on each. This should include the name of the child, address, telephone, parents' name, age and date of birth, and space for other information which you will collect during the year (such as interests and hobbies). The date of birth is kept by many directors so a card of congratulations can be sent or the names listed in a choir paper each month. The information on the card should also indicate whether or not the child has sung in another choir, whether he plays the piano or other instrument, and something of the quality of the voice.

At registration time it is wise to hear the child's voice, even if you have heard it the year before. The director needs to know how the voice is developing, and in the case of boys, signs of voice change should be noted. With the smaller children one needs to observe pitch problems and tonal memory. A short pattern of two or three notes will indicate much of this. If a voice test is given it should be very simple, and perhaps the word "audition" or "test" should not be mentioned since it can frighten away timid children. The test should come only after you have talked with the child and made him feel relaxed and at ease. A good approach is to ask the child to sing a song he knows without any help from the piano. Sometimes the child cannot think of a song because of the newness and strangeness of the place, so you should have some titles to suggest such as "My Country, 'Tis of Thee," or a song which you know has been taught in the church school. You may have to start singing with the child at first until he loses his self-consciousness. Then try a five note scale pattern such as *f, g, a, b* flat, *c* (up or down) on "loo" or "lah." With the very young child it seems easier to come down the scale. If the child cannot do this, try to get him to match a single tone which you sing first. If he still does not do well there is no real cause for alarm.

If the child cannot reproduce any pitch you give, reverse the procedure and match the pitch he is able to sing. Then see if he can move away from the first pitch. Almost all children will be able to do this, but their stage fright may keep you from getting a true picture of their ability. What you really want to discover is whether the child can match a pitch and whether his ear is keen or not. In the meantime you will discover a little about the tone quality which will improve with work in the choir.

One warning about the audition: by no means let the child sense any concern on your part about his ability to sing. If the child does not sing well, does not match any tone you sing, cannot sing alone or with you, do not let him know that you find this unusual. Do not get flustered, excited, and upset, but stay relaxed. The child who has difficulty probably has had little experience with music at home, and a little training is all that is necessary. Sometimes it is just a case of not finding the head voice—the child speaks instead of singing. Time will solve most problems and the child whose voice does not move correctly and freely to different pitches will usually blossom rather quickly in the choir.

It is the director's job to help each individual achieve his highest potential. He should not discourage those who may seem to have lesser vocal talents. Too many directors are impatient with singers of undeveloped skills and wish to spend all their time in the preparation of anthems, using only the best trained singers. Helping all singers is particularly important in working with small children, for most of them begin choir experience much as a baby takes his first step.

Over the years the director will need to keep a record of the vocal weaknesses or characteristics of each child, for it is difficult at times to keep tab on a large number of children if there are several choirs. These records will give the needed information which can help you to help the children with vocal problems. You can also see what progress is being made from year to year. The record of course is private and no one else should see it. If children should see your comments about other voices real harm could be done.

Some directors do not use any voice test with the very small children (ages five and six) but merely take the group as it is in order to draw out everyone's participation. Many small children are timid and would do so poorly that the test would mean little. The testing can be done in the first meeting of the group by singing "Hello" on different pitches to each child with the child answering "Hello" on the pitch sung to him. A downward pattern is easiest to follow. The director can learn to tell whether a little child is going to sing the "Hello" comfortably and easily by observing the face (is it eager or worried?). Whatever happens the director should smile encouragingly and move on to the next child so each child feels that he has been successful in this attempt. Allow for timidity on the first try, and the next time there will be less possibility of failure in matching pitches.

The Primary Choir

CHAPTER V

WHILE THERE ARE SOME CHURCHES WITH CHOIRS for children four years of age and even three, the musical results leave much to be desired and there is a tendency to think of them as "the cute little things"—even going so far as to call them the cherub choir. A choir for three-year-olds is little more than a nursery, and it is preferable that their musical experiences come in the church-school program rather than in a separately organized choir. If four-year-olds are organized into a choir, the approach would be similar to that for five-year-olds since both are about the same level of development. Let us think of the primary choir as a combination of five- and six-year-olds in one group, and seven- and eight-year-olds in another. They may be referred to as Primary 1 and Primary 2.

As indicated earlier the six- and eight-year-olds do not work well together, and it is difficult to use materials and techniques that fit both ages. If you work at one level the other is confused, bored, or tired, and there will be problems of discipline. A thirty-minute period is long enough for the five- and six-year-olds, and even this must be handled very carefully with plenty of variety since young children cannot remain still for a long period of time. Their attention span is very short, and they cannot concentrate on one thing for any great length of time. With the seven- and eight-year-olds a forty- or forty-five-minute period can be used. The attention span here is still short, and the work must include many varied approaches. Since one approach is through rhythmic games and activities the need for adequate space for these will indicate the size of rehearsal room needed and perhaps the maximum number of children feasible in the choir. There should be room for the children to move around, to march, to skip, and to enjoy rhythmic games. If there is room for the children to lie down on a rug for a short rest that too may be helpful. It is wiser to divide into several small groups than to have one large group which is difficult or impossible to handle.

For both Primary 1 and Primary 2 the program will need Action, with a capital "A." Keep the rehearsal moving, going from activity to activity quickly. It means you will not stay very long at any one thing, in fact, only as long as the children show interest. On some days the group can concentrate better than other days. On rainy, dark, gloomy days the children will have shorter spans of attention and this will call for added variety in their program. From three to five minutes is about as long as you can spend on any one project. If you are using a game which will be repeated in the future, have only a few children play it, then move quickly to something else. The next week another group can have their turn, and the game stays fresh because of anticipation.

Much time must go into planning the rehearsal. There are so many possible procedures that the director must choose materials and methods carefully. Study the music to be learned and decide how each number can best be presented. Go over rhythmic games, study of intervals, notations, hymns, and stories and decide which will be best for the day. When the rehearsal begins, make things hum by moving quickly from one thing to the next. If there is hesitation on your part, disciplinary problems are apt to come up —and the fault is with the director and not the child.

PRIMARY I

The choir of five- and six-year-olds is more of a preparatory choir than a functioning choir, for most of your actual work with them will consist of ear training. Many children will have had singing experience in their homes, but many more will have had little or none. Some will have no concept of pitch, and time will be spent in games and songs to develop this. As you work on the pitch sense you will also work on rhythmic response, for if a child can keep a pitch but has no sense of rhythm he will not make a good choir member.

The material you choose should be simple, yet attractive. The music must be melodic and appealing to the child. Only the melody should be used, with your voice setting the pattern. Some directors use a flute or violin for patterning. If the piano is used, only the melody should be played—the addition of harmony clouds the

42

melody so the child flounders. The songs will contain only simple intervals, and should indicate the same feeling as the words—that is, a joyous tune should be matched with joyous words. See that the accents agree in both music and words. Not all of the materials on the market have a good matching of words and music. Sometimes church literature is chosen with the words in mind for a specific teaching purpose and the music is "picked up" somewhere or hammered out by a writer with little imagination and less understanding of children and music.

The words should be within the comprehension of the children, or else they should be easy to explain. Words of many syllables are not good at this age. The texts should deal with things which have an appeal—nature; other people; God; Jesus as a friend of children; home, with its joy and warmth; the Church, with its joyful experiences; action songs; holidays, such as Christmas and Easter (and even Halloween, which historically has a tie with the Church). The range is much larger than one would imagine.

An illustration of a good choice of Primary 1 song is titled "Before Dinner" and is found in *The Whole World Singing*. It is about the Belgian Congo and is useful in teaching about foreign lands. The song tells of the mother and child getting dinner and how they raise the corn and pound it into powder to make meal. It is an attractive song with much repetition, which makes it easy to teach. With this song the children can imitate the sound of drums by cupping the hands and clapping. Perhaps the boys can be the drummers while the girls sing.

Another kind of song which is very effective with the small child is the question and answer song. From the book, *Songs for Early Childhood*, children enjoy the song, "Who Made the Stars in the Bright Blue Sky?" The answer is, "God our Father." The next part, "Who made the birds and bees that fly?" is answered

43

by "God, our loving Father." This song could be introduced by talking about something familiar and beautiful, then asking who made this beautiful thing. The question leads easily into the thought and the words of the song before the children begin to learn it. Then say, "I am going to sing some questions, and the first question will be answered with 'God our Father,' and the second with 'God, our loving Father.' We will see if you can give the right answer." Sing the answer first yourself, then ask the children to sing it with you. After the leader sings the question, a few will try the answers. The next week some will still remember the answers, and in a few weeks the entire group will be able to participate. Another way to teach question and answer songs is to divide the group, with one half singing the question and the other half singing the answer.

It is only a short step from this kind of song to creative work. You can say, "Let's make up some questions which we could answer with the answers of our song," and they will be full of ideas which can be sung to the tune of the song. One little boy made up these: "Who made the baby, baby dear?" and "Who made our mother and father dear?" The choir feels a great deal of pride when they make up songs of their own.

At first the children will need guidance, for making up songs will be a new experience. During the fall my choir children talked about the changing seasons, and a few knew that another word for fall was "autumn." To the question, "What do we have in the fall?" one child answered, "Bad colds!" This was hardly the direction to take for the song, but we used this as a starting point and for two weeks added ideas for a song about autumn. Naturally there was something about the leaves changing color and falling to the ground. The result was a fine song and a creative experience.

In addition to songs based on experience, we have tried to create

44

songs built on Bible verses and stories. The small children can make simple hymns, and the older children do very well in this field.

Children like songs in which some phrases are set for them and which provide opportunity for them to add sentences out of their own experience. Such a song is "The Lord Has Done Great Things for Us." [1] They sing together the first phrase and then take turns telling of some "great thing," such as seeing the first spring flowers, a sunset, or a new baby, before singing the last phrase.

As we turn now to musical training, there is one vocal problem which you will undoubtedly meet with the small child. Many will sing in a high, piping voice. This can be lowered by having them imitate sounds with which they are familiar, such as a fire engine siren or a deep bell. When there is only one child who needs help, it is best not to spend more than a few seconds or a minute with the individual. If too much time is spent on one individual you will lose the other children's attention. In all cases the child should not be made to feel that he is being singled out for doing something wrong.

Many five- and six-year-olds cannot sing a melody line "in tune" with others, and we quite wrongly call these children monotones. There are many reasons why children are not able to sing in tune, but it is interesting to note that children from homes where there is family musical participation usually sing well at an early age.

When a child has difficulty in matching a single tone sung by the director, the director should match the tone the child is singing. Usually they can then proceed together for at least one or two pitch changes. Moving the body in accord with words sung—such as high-low, short-tall, down-up—will help many children move from pitch to pitch. Imitating an elevator is a good way to get the

[1] *Hymns for Primary Worship.*

45

child up and down the scale accurately. Draw a line on the blackboard to indicate an express elevator. This will provide a visual aid for rising or descending, and the child should sing "oo" to imitate the elevator as he goes from top to bottom or bottom to top. After accuracy in pitch from one to eight is established, the elevator may become a local, with stops at three and five.

I have found that if I can get the children to look me directly in the eye they will match pitches more easily. If one of your children has a problem with pitch, try to stand directly in front of him as he sings. If you stand too far away, there is a tendency for the mind and voice to wander. I recall one child who sang well if I stood in front of her, but if I stood away from her any distance at all, her eyes would wander and her voice would drop from the pitch line. When the children sang as a group, I tried to arrange the choir so that I stood exactly in front of her where I could keep her attention.

All of this indicates that pitch problems are sometimes just a matter of concentration, both with primaries and with older children. One of the first tasks of the choir director is to train children to listen, and this is not as easy as it may seem. Children may be attentive and still not listen. They may even be very much interested in what they are hearing but still not listen carefully to it. Therefore, careful guidance is needed. Asking children to close their eyes as they listen helps them to concentrate.

The poor singer should always be encouraged to keep singing, and must never feel that he is being censured. It is much more important that the child be happy in his musical participation than it is for him to sing perfectly. Many a child has been retarded in his musical development—even permanently stunted—by learning that his singing is "different." With some work on the director's part, most so-called monotone problems can be solved.

As a part of the musical education of the child it is well to begin teaching something about notation and the symbols of music. Our choir has a set of cards which includes all kinds of notes—whole, half, quarter, eighth, sixteenth. There are also such symbols as a sharp, a flat, a natural, treble clef, bass clef, and the kinds of rests. The children begin by identifying the various kinds of notes as the cards are held up. The first session is devoted to giving the names of a few of the notes. The second week the names are repeated, and then a flash card session of a few seconds indicates how much is remembered. The third week some of the children will be able to give the names without prompting. As the weeks go by additional cards should be added, but the children will tire quickly if you use this device too long at any rehearsal. For variety I sometimes place the cards on a music stand by the piano and ask a child to choose the card which shows a certain note value. Or I have them close their eyes and I put a card in each hand. When the eyes are opened I ask the person holding a given symbol to stand and show it to the choir—so the choir can decide whether it is correct or not. As they become more sure of themselves you can have the children match a note with its corresponding rest. We also use various games including the basket game in which children draw from a box or basket slips of paper which tell them what to do—"find the half rest," "the whole rest."

Let us go now to rhythm, for a great deal of attention and time should be given to it at this particular age level. Children are lively and movement is natural. Most of them have a strong desire to participate in rhythmic exercises but many are not able to do them well. Many who are poor at first will improve by observing others —children learn rapidly from each other. Imitation is the best device here, but there are certain songs that call for a definite rhythmic response, such as a rocking motion. Even small boys at this age are perfectly willing and happy to join the girls in rocking a doll in rhythm to music.

Boys particularly enjoy being buoys in the water. In the summer they see buoys rocking from side to side in the water, and they enjoy rocking with the music. Sometimes it is a game of tugboats —chug, chug, chugging along. Trains gathering speed and then slowing down are suggestive of accelerando and ritard.

Children also enjoy acting the part of animals. A boy becomes an elephant by bending his body over and swinging one arm in front for the long trunk. Or they can act out the part of flying birds or hopping rabbits. The limit of animals and actions depends upon your imagination and that of the children.

Of course some rhythms invite clapping or drum beating. Clapping is easiest to do since no time is needed for distributing materials, but the children can make drums of many materials. Rhythm sticks are simply made by sawing long dowels into proper lengths.

Action will automatically come with certain songs which have a strong rhythmic pulse. Last year we were preparing for a Christmas program when we were to have a visiting Hand Bell Choir from Washington. While the children in the choir were not to sing with the bells, we talked about the bells and how they are played. Then we pretended we had hand bells in our hands, and we sang our Christmas song with hands swinging the bells in the rhythm of the song. At first some of the children had to watch the leader to get the pattern, and some were not able to sing and swing at the same time. The wise director will be on the lookout for songs which lend themselves to rhythmic activity. Beware of songs with stylized motions which have little or no relation to the words (as suggested in so many collections of songs for small children). Keep your eyes and mind open for songs which can be used with meaningful action and let the children help you with the interpretation.

Some songbooks for children add several pages of piano music which may be played for rhythmic activities. Two good books are *Creative Rhythmic Movement for Children* by Gladys Andrews and *Illustrated Games and Rhythms for Children* by Frank H. Geri.

Thus far we have talked of action as a teaching device, but action is also useful in changing the pace of the rehearsal. Children are not able to sit still for long, so the director must plan for many spots of action (or inaction) as relaxation. One game children enjoy is sitting and pretending they are rag dolls. Or if you have plenty of space they can lie on the floor as limp dolls. Sometimes dropping the arms down and dropping the head gives needed rest from mental and physical activity.

The dramatization of a song can be an original experience and a valuable interpretive one and should be used with the very small child. At all times the imagination of the child should be depended on for guidance, and the child should be encouraged to suggest ways of interpretation.

Children like songs and games that test their imagination. If you are teaching a new song ask them to suggest ways to help understand the song and what it is about. There is a little song, "Butterflies," which children like to sing. It tells about the butterfly's going to different flowers, and it may be acted out by having a garden with hollyhocks, roses, and any other flowers the children suggest. Then a certain number of children are butterflies and fly from flower to flower. The end of the song says,

> "Butterfly, butterfly, home is the best;
> Fold your wings gently and rest." [2]

[2] From *Songs for Early Childhood.* Copyright, 1958, W. L. Jenkins. Used by permission.

49

Instead of giving instructions, leave all of the action to the children. At the last words they usually fold their arms quietly and sink down to the floor.

One of the first songs learned in the fall may be "Autumn Leaves." [3] Freedom of movement is encouraged as the words "softly floating down" and "fall the leaves" are sung. Other easy songs for dramatization are "Who Has Seen the Wind?," "Wake Up, Little Flowers," and "Going to Sleep," all in the same book. [4]

A favorite song of many children tells the story of the birth of Jesus and each stanza ends with "Alleluia, praise the Christ, and sing to God, His Father." [5] When these words occur the children lift the arms and heads in a gesture of adoration and praise.

At the very first rehearsal with the little children I begin to talk about how wonderful it is to belong to a choir and how happy we are that they belong to it. I spend some time telling them the name of their choir so they learn the name and recognize it. Every boy and girl present feels that he or she belongs to the choir and the name means something personally.

From this we move to the idea that as members of the choir they have a special name. They are called "choristers." There are several marks of a good chorister and certain rules that he must follow.

These rules are printed on small cards and are given to every new child each year. They are to be learned during the week, and everyone says them together the following week. During successive weeks they are reviewed in different ways—the director starting one and the child finishing, different children saying different rules,

[3] *Song for Early Childhood.*

[4] *God's Wonderful World.*

[5] *We Go to Church.*

50

and other ways which seem best. One effective game we have used is the basket game referred to previously.

PRIMARY 2

The Primary 2 choir, of course, can take on more work and more intensive study than can the Primary 1, provided they have had the experiences which were discussed in part one of this chapter. If the group is new, however, then the teaching process should start with the earlier material already suggested. This choir will use the same type of song material as Primary 1, but they can now learn longer songs and can move more freely among wider intervals.

With older primaries singing has become a natural and easy expression of everyday living. Emma Dickson Sheehy, in *There's Music in Children,* says: "Small children use music in a functional way and we are likely to educate it out of them. They sing about their play, about going to bed, etc. Unfortunately, but for obvious reasons, they lose this natural ability as they get older, for children do what others do, and older people do not go around singing in this fashion." They will sing easily, naturally, and they will make the lilt of the song fit the mood.

You can now start your choir to work on learning intervals, perhaps making use of a ladder drawn on the blackboard. From the first rung to the third rung gives a visual aid to the singing of a third. I also use the elevator idea, for most children enjoy riding in an elevator. I draw a box on the blackboard and put some lines across to indicate the first floor, second floor, and on up. Then the children start on the elevator and go up to the fifth floor, singing "loo" for each level. Then we take the express elevator which comes from the fifth to the first floor without stopping on the way. This calls for thinking how the first floor note will sound before starting down. Then the choir tries to see how it would

51

sound if it went from one to three without stopping at two. The picture of the ladder or the elevator helps the child to see what he is doing instead of having to imagine it. Point to the picture as you explain the intervals—the third, the fifth, and then the more difficult intervals.

After the group has had a good deal of experience with intervals you may move on to the difference between major and minor. It takes a long time before all children can recognize the difference immediately. I do not use the idea that major is glad and minor is sad, for I do not think this is true. It is really a matter of the arrangement of the two thirds in a triad—and many an older person is unable to recognize this easily.

At this age the children are becoming alert to rhythmic and melodic patterns, since they have been taught to fit words and tunes together. The text already indicates to them whether the song should be sung quickly or slowly, whether it should be loud or soft, whether it is a song of joy or quietness.

One of the hymns we used was "In Bethlehem, 'Neath Starlit Skies." The choir learned the "Alleluias" which end each phrase except the third. This became a game, for the children had to be alert not to sing "Alleluia" after the third line. Next they learned the words of the hymn. After a few weeks I asked some questions about the hymn to see how much the children remembered and how much of the story they had absorbed. We tried to think what happened in Bethlehem, what kind of night it was, the town mentioned in the song, what time of day it was, and similar questions. This drew out of them the words of the song and etched them more deeply in their memory. Next I drew a long line on the blackboard to indicate the first line with the two "Alleluias." Then I asked if the pattern was the same for the second line, and the choir agreed that it was. When we got to the third line I said that this must be like the first and second, and there were loud "Nos." So we stopped to see how it was different. This type of approach fixed the melodic pattern firmly in their minds. Then we returned to the meaning of "Alleluia" and the joyous story which the song told.

This choir will also begin to study more difficult rhythmic patterns by clapping them. Rhythm instruments can be used more easily and effectively at this age level, and it is at this age that I begin to have them read the patterns from notation on the black-board. In the earlier choir they have learned to recognize note values and most of the rests. Now we begin to extend this by practice in reading rhythmic notation. I place on the blackboard a metrical pattern of quarter notes and quarter rests. These patterns are always at first in three quarter or four quarter time and since each example has quarter notes as the basic movement, the children clap their hands for every quarter note and rest for every quarter note rest. We see how many beats there are in each measure—whether three or four—and this helps them understand the meaning of 4/4 and 3/4 time signatures. When the children can clap the rhythm correctly I play something on the piano which uses the same rhythmic pattern of notes and rests while they clap their hands in rhythm. Next I play something different from their pattern but keep them clapping the original pattern. The children can pretend that they are clapping the singing part while I play the accompaniment. This helps to develop an independence from the accompaniment, often different rhythmically from the voice part.

At first I put only a few measures on the blackboard, but soon I move on to the presentation of several rows of measures so the children learn to move from the end of one line to the beginning of the next. When they have learned to clap almost any kind of pattern I put two different patterns on the blackboard, one above the other, and have all children clap each pattern until it is perfect. Then the group is divided into two, and the two patterns are clapped simultaneously so the children can learn to stay on their own part without being distracted by the others. Gradually a third line can be introduced and similarly used.

This study of rhythm patterns leads into sight reading. From the flash card exercises the children have learned to recognize note values. Now, as they clap the rhythms, you should have them sing "loo" on each note. When this becomes monotonous, suggest that these "loo's" can be made higher or lower in tone, and that this is the way they learn to recognize a tune. Draw a staff on the blackboard and put in the notes of a very simple tune. Hum each note at you point to it, then have the children hum with you. Then change to another simple tune using different notes and have the children practice sounding each note as you point to it. Of necessity, the first tunes you use must be very simple, but as the children learn to associate the sight of intervals with their sounds, music sight reading is on its way.

We begin in this choir to study musical instruments. We learn the names, the families (strings, woodwinds, brass, percussion), and the kind of tone of each. After the children are familiar with instruments and can recognize note values, we form a little rhythm orchestra. I have used *Eighteen Folk Tunes for Children's Rhythm Bands* by Virginia P. Churchill but any simple pattern can be written out. Base your patterns on music which can be played on the piano while the children beat the rhythms. The children enjoy turning the chairs around and using them as music racks, with several children reading from one "music stand" and one book.

At Christmas time we use bells, which I encourage the children to bring from home, and we sing all kinds of songs which can use bells in rhythm with the words. We use pictures of bell ringers and bell choirs and talk about the ancient art of handbell ringing. At first the choristers try ringing a bell with only one hand, and then with both hands. Since each bell the children bring rings differently it takes a little practice to get them sounding at one time. All this helps to extend rhythmic control. Pitch perception may also be stimulated by bell ringing.

One of our most successful long time projects with the seven- and eight-year-olds was a study of various birds. The purpose of this particular project was to sharpen the listening perception of the children and to add opportunity for creative song making. There are many available songs about birds, but we also made up our own. Each of the children began a collection of index cards, on which were pasted stickers showing different birds. The dime store produced a book about birds which gave us a start. There are also some fine recordings from Cornell University of various bird songs. The use of these records was a boon to ear training.

Next we secured a little book by Coit and Bampton called *Let's Listen to the Birds,* and this had several motifs that could be played on the piano. The children soon learned to recognize these. From various sources I secured pictures of birds. These were used for visual recognition. This soon turned into a game of listening to the recording of a bird song and then matching the song with the right picture. The children made particular study of the robin, the cardinal, the goldfinch, the bluebird, and the woodpecker—a wonderful bird for rhythm study.

The blackboard is an indispensable piece of equipment for this choir, for it gives many opportunities for activity and change of pace. Games to develop pitch consciousness and games to develop dynamics will be best presented visually on the board.

One popular game with the choir is called "Near and Far." On the blackboard several children draw a large box beside a big circle. Two notes—such as middle *c* and the *c* two octaves above—are then played on the piano. Or it may be middle *c* with *d* just above it. If the notes are far apart the children are to place an X in the box. If the notes are close together the X goes in the circle. The musical examples should be played rather rapidly so close attention and fast decisions are called for. The children enjoy this type of ear training.

After hurricane Diane came through Virginia several years ago I drew some houses on the blackboard and we talked about the storm. I said, "Do you remember how the wind blew and how the rain came down? Sometimes it came very, very hard and the wind blew so loudly that the rain sounded louder than ever. Then when the wind stopped for a little while the rain came more softly. Now, I am going to make loud hurricane rain on the piano, and then I am going to make soft hurricane rain and I want you to make the same kind of rain on the blackboard that I play on the piano." The children made bold stripes of rain when the piano played loud chords, and small slashes of rain when softer chords were sounded. Not only did the children have to listen closely, but they were at the same time having a lesson in dynamics.

Rhythms can also have dynamic differences, and we use drumbeats which are loud and soft to teach the difference. The children can use the chairs as drums. Or they can draw heavy and light slashes on the blackboard to indicate differences. It is important at this point that you teach accent. Make sets of four notes and indicate the need for a loud drumbeat on the first beat and softer beats on the second, third, and fourth. Then practice the same thing with either the sound of horses or marching feet approaching from a distance. This gives practice in crescendo and diminuendo. This should of course be done without the piano playing since the teacher must listen to see if the sound is right.

At this age I like to start letting the children handle the hymnals of the church, and we make quite an event of it. I take some time to talk about the hymnbook and explain that it is one of our most important books in the church. It has all of the songs we like to sing, especially those which are used in the worship service. It has songs which can be sung at home too. I mention some of the hymns which can be sung as grace before meals or as prayers at bedtime.

Next we learn how to take the hymnal from the rack carefully —not tearing or pulling it out. Of course we talk about the proper handling of the book—we do not throw it down or drop it on the floor. Then I place the number of a familiar hymn on the blackboard and ask the choir to find the place in the book while I am playing the hymn. Some children will be slower than others and can be helped by other children nearby.

Then we talk about the hymn. The choice should be a fairly familiar one since the reading of the text will not be too rapid. Children need to be taught how to follow the words of any given stanza from line to line, and a familiar hymn such as "For the Beauty of the Earth" helps them to find the right places because of their familiarity with the words. I usually say something like this: "Now I want to show you how we sing this hymn. We go across this line. Then, instead of reading the next line directly underneath, in a hymnal we come down to the next group of lines and read there." Then we sing the hymn with the children singing largely from memory but also experiencing the excitement of following the right words. It is the beginning of a habit which must be learned. I find it necessary to repeat this several times so the children are sure what I mean and know where to look for the next words. It perhaps is wise to teach a hymn without the book first so their first look at the book will be a pleasurable experience of recognition.

Another job is teaching the children how to stand properly and walk in processional holding the hymnals correctly. How does our choir stand when ready to sing in church? How do they walk down the aisle? How do they hold their books? Then I show the children how to hold the book in the palm of the left hand while the right hand balances it. It is not easy for a small child to hold a hymnal at first, but he likes to try. After they practice walking and standing with the hymnals, I have them sing a hymn, which they locate. Afterwards they are asked to put the books away properly. Handling the hymnal becomes something important and special. Since the book is not used every rehearsal it is something to be looked forward to. I also make it a point to check hands for cleanliness before working with hymnals.

At first most of the hymns we learn from the hymnal are taught by rote, but the very simple act of holding the hymnal while singing is a step in the right direction. The next step is to encourage the children to try to locate the places in the church service when everybody takes a hymnal and stands to sing. At first they are confused, but they soon follow the example of the adults and learn to find the numbers in time to join the singing. A habit is thus formed that prepares them for one of the procedures of a worship service so they can take their places in the service with a minimum of difficulty.

The public schools have made wide use of music appreciation and listening to records, and the primary choir should do likewise—centering the experience in the field of church music. Some of the music may be quiet listening music, or perhaps some will be used as a teaching device. For example use the "Pastoral Symphony" from *The Messiah* by Handel when preparing the children for a quiet song about Christmas Eve. This could be tied in with the familiar carol, "Silent Night"—the beautiful, holy night when

Christ was born. Since the listening span is short you will not use all of the recording but merely enough to set the mood for the children. When used with a picture the music makes a definite impression.

Also use recordings to teach the child to use imagination when listening to music. Have the child listen for the mood of the music, to try to understand what the music is trying to say. Have them tell whether the music is gay, sad, quiet, or busy. Children need to be trained to listen discerningly to music—not merely to listen for pretty sounds. It takes time to awaken this perception in listening, so you should ask pertinent questions if the children seem to be vague at first.

In this day of radio and television, when we are constantly being bombarded with sound, many people have become so accustomed to a background of sound that they do not actually listen at all. I believe we need to train children to really listen to music. This means piano and instrumental music as well as vocal. Occasionally it would be well to take the children into the sanctuary and let them hear something played on the church organ, so they will come to recognize the sound of an organ. This involves explaining the various stops as well as playing selections from organ literature. Also encourage children to attend special concerts and programs which will be of interest to them.

What we are saying is that a choir program is built on a variety of experiences. We often get the idea that a choir is a place for singing only. A choir is a group which must be trained in musical matters and musical language; the more it is trained the more musical it becomes. So the choir rehearsal should touch on many aspects of the whole field of music—not just on songs alone.

Very occasionally (since it takes a great deal of time) I have the children listen carefully to a recording. Then I pass out construction paper and crayons and ask them to draw a picture of the music they were listening to. What did they think about as they listened? Interesting results come from combining the graphic and aural arts. I have also asked the children to draw a picture of their favorite song. One of the best I ever received had the bottom half of the page colored green and the top half blue with yellow stars. I did not know what it was, and the child thought it very strange that I did not recognize "Silent Night." It really was a good interpretation, for there was nothing but stars in the sky and everything was quiet—nothing to disturb the calm and peace.

I recall another instance when a child struggled long and hard to illustrate "Fairest Lord Jesus" with a picture. She just could not get it to please her, so she asked me if I thought it looked right. I said, "Yes, I think that is quite all right. No one living in the world today really knows exactly what Jesus looked like. We have lots of pictures of what painters think he looked like, but no one really knows for sure. Perhaps your picture is just as good as some other person's. I think it is very fine."

Let us sum up now the work with the seven- and eight-year-olds. We should give them ear and rhythm training, opportunity to do creative song making, better music appreciation, and of course singing. To keep these various activities as interesting as possible the director must constantly find new ways to introduce material. Think of ways that will help the children understand what they are doing so that they are not learning by note alone all the time. It is very easy to teach the children some of the harder songs if the director arranges ahead of time for some activity that is interesting to the child. Enthusiasm is aroused and the child looks forward to the frequent repetition of material in varied ways and approaches. But if you always use the approach, "I will sing the song to you and

you sing it back to me," the child will get tired of the song before
it is learned.

Keep the rehearsals moving; do not allow any lags. In all rehearsals
know what you are going to do, and when. Move from one thing
quickly into another so there is no indecision on your part. This
means that everything is planned and in readiness when rehearsal
begins. See that the music for the accompanist is on the piano and
that any pictures or other materials to be used are at your finger
tips.

Finally we might mention that children will get the proper attitude toward choir, singing, and the church from your attitude. If
your enthusiasm shows, the child will be enthusiastic. They want
to imitate you and will give back to you a picture of yourself. You
will be teaching habits of reverence, habits of worship, habits of
work, careful workmanship, the ability to concentrate on the job
at hand, and other fine qualities. By the time the children are
ready to leave the primary choir they should have learned to be on
time, to be regular in attendance, to have respect for the church and
for their vestments. They will know how to handle the hymnal
carefully and will respect it as a book of value. They are now ready
for the junior choir.

The Junior Choir

 THERE IS A WORLD OF DIFFERENCE BETWEEN THE primary and junior child. The primary child is still a very little child in many ways. He is dependent upon his home and his family, and yet he is beginning to explore the larger world. From nine on he becomes more of an individual with a distinct personality. Physically, the legs get longer although the torso remains about the same. Muscular control develops rapidly and hands become skillful in fashioning all sorts of things. The girls are usually larger than the boys and seem to grow faster at this age. Mentally, the attention span is much longer and juniors can work more extensively on a project. They are eager to learn and are full of creative ideas. They want to know everything and to learn everything they possibly can. They are much like sponges, absorbing an amazing amount of material.

Surprisingly enough the junior child is a perfectionist. He wants things to be right. For this reason you must be careful not to present the junior choir in any service unless they can do a good job and will feel confident of themselves. Any unhappy experience in singing an anthem puts a damper on their desire to try again.

It is at this age that I divide the boys and girls, although I know there are many directors who do not. I do this for a number of reasons. The boys and girls are beginning to be very much aware of each other. The boys are interested in the girls but do not want the girls to know it, and the reverse is true. This causes a good bit of friction. It is amusing to observe, but for the children it is serious. The girls say they cannot stand the boys, all the time wanting their notice. And the boys tease the girls and pick at them —anything to aggravate them and attract attention to themselves, though they are not conscious of that motive. All this means lost time at rehearsals.

When I have worked with the boys and girls together I have found it best to place the boys in the front rows of the choir with the girls behind. I always call them "fellows," never "boys," and tell them I have them in front because there are so many times I need their help. When they are close at hand I do not mind asking them to help me. And I do give them jobs—getting books for me and other legitimate jobs which show that I really do need their help. There is also less trouble with the girls in this seating arrangement, and the boys do not have opportunity to tease them.

Another reason for separating the boys and girls is that in rehearsal I can present the work differently. I can appeal to the girls along one line in introducing new music, whereas I will not necessarily want or be able to use the same teaching method with the boys. Illustrations for each group may be entirely different. One explanation will appeal to the feminine—another to the masculine.

The most important reason in my mind for the separation is that with two separate choirs I reach more boys. Junior boys are reaching the stage where they may think it is sissy or effeminate to sing. Unthinking people further this by suggesting that the "Y" program or football should be the only activity for boys. If the boys have their own choir organization it has more appeal for them than a combined choir.

To encourage the idea of a choir for boys tell them about the many fine boy choirs around the world such as the Vienna Boy Choir, the Little Singers of Paris, the Columbus Boy Choir, the Appollo Boy Choir, and others. Tell about the many Episcopal churches where only boys and men provide the music. Play recordings of boy choirs or take the group to hear a visiting choir in concert.

To promote the idea of the choir's being a "masculine" organization get various groups of men in the church interested in doing things with the boys. The men of the young adult fellowship of some churches have arranged hikes, picnics, fishing trips, and outings with the boys. Many of the group are fathers of the boys, and they do the organizing. The mothers provide the picnic lunch, wave goodby, and send the "men" on their way. In other years the male section of the adult choir has helped. I recall one year when the men of the choir took the boys to a football game. I have also on occasion combined the men and boys to sing for a Sunday service, much in the cathedral tradition. The boys sang the soprano and alto parts, and the blend was beautiful.

Some of the boys in my junior choir are a little older than the girls since they start in at the age of nine and continue until their voices change. Here again it is easier to hold the boys when they are not with the girls. Boys can be extremely sensitive about their changing, unreliable voices. With the boys alone you can discuss very frankly the problems of voice change, and the boys accept the bobbles without any particular notice or embarrassment.

I realize that some educators will say that boys and girls should be together, that they should be learning to get along with each other. I am sure the viewpoint is justifiable, and I am in hearty accord with it, but I do not believe that one hour a week spent in separate rehearsals will cause any great Freudian frustrations. I do know that much better choir results are obtained by the separation in rehearsals.

In general the boys and girls learn the same music separately but sing together in church. In some cases they do learn different music. For example, the boys sing carols which particularly appeal to them and the girls sing other types such as lullabies. In church on Sunday the boys and girls walk together in the processional side by side. When we first began having the children sing every Sunday the only logical seating arrangement was to have the choirs seated in the front pews on either side of the center aisle. In order to get all the boys on one side and all the girls together on the other it was easier to have a line of boys beside a line of girls, although it could be done by having each choir grouped together.

I went to the boys first. They had been practicing processing for several weeks, so I said to them, "You may do the processional as you choose—you may come down, fellows together, with the girls' choir in front of your choir, or you may come down a fellow and a girl." Immediately they said, "We don't want to walk with any old girls." This was the reaction I had expected, so I said, "You don't have to walk with the girls, and it makes no difference to me. I just suggested it because the adult choir does it that way—the men walking beside the women—and it looks very nice. I thought if you wanted to do the same thing you could. But if you don't want to that is perfectly all right." At that point, to allow this suggestion to percolate, I turned to the piano and was quite busy with something else for a few moments. When I turned around they had thought it over and one boy who was spokesman for the group said, "Well, I guess if the grown-up people do it we can too." "Oh no," I protested, "it doesn't make a bit of difference. If you would rather walk by yourselves that is perfectly all right." "No," he said, "We will try it that way. We want to do like the adult choir does." I tried exactly the same thing on the girls and got the same reaction. And the processional has worked out that way through the years.

We should now talk about the use of the junior boys and girls in the service—how they can be used and why they should be used. I am a strong advocate of having them in the service every Sunday if at all possible. At present our church has no junior church service, so the children are not in another worship service. We do not have an extended church school program, so the children are free to be in the morning worship service. I strongly feel that the children can begin to be a part of the worship service every Sunday with good results for them and for the church.

I do not feel it is enough to have the boys and girls come in occasionally to sing. When you do that you are making a spectacle of the choirs. They are on exhibition and are really "showing off" instead of contributing to the service of worship. Children sense this and consequently do not do their best singing. The choir is often put in a conspicuous spot unfairly, and it is difficult for the children to act as a choir should. I think they should be in service every Sunday to learn to be a part of the service. The children need to be trained to take part in worship and the best way to teach this is to have the choirs participate consistently with the feeling that they have prepared for and are making a real contribution to the service.

One of the advantages of the choir program is that you are educating the adults through the children. Many adults have no sense of what is right and what is wrong in a service. They have gone to church all their lives, stood up and sat down, prayed here, sung there, listened to the sermon, without any real understanding of what they are doing or why. Once the choir members understand the mechanics of worship they will help educate their parents. You will then have a better trained and more sensitive congregation. So we train the children who in turn train their elders. But first the director must know all about the ordering of worship.

Each denomination develops its distinctive pattern of worship and the wise director studies all of these. You need, however, to know the pattern in your own church best of all. For example, I am working in a Methodist church. John Wesley was the founder, and he and his compatriots instinctively followed a standard order of worship, since they were members of the Church of England with its rich liturgy. As set out by Wesley it is a fairly formal service, following a very definite pattern. There are several possible variations in the various orders in *The Methodist Hymnal,* and there is always the privilege of making further changes. The children will gain by studying the various orders in the hymnal and comparing them with the one in actual use. While there is value in talking about the reasons for each part of the service, the real value comes from participating with understanding week after week.

In our service people are for the most part quiet during the organ prelude. The children are dumbfounded when they hear anybody talk during the prelude, for they understand why there is organ music as people enter the church. They sometimes criticize the ushers, some of whom tend to be talkative in the narthex.

Hymns take on new meaning in their worship setting, and each week we rehearse the hymns to be sung the following Sunday. I give information about hymns, but rehearsal time is too short to talk very much about all of them. I choose one each week for special attention, discussing the tune, the poet, the historical setting, or other items which will make the hymn more interesting.

The children should be rehearsed in the responsive readings. Many are not easy, and some use difficult words or ideas. We practice these each week, and each child has a chance during the year to be the minister and read the alternate verses. It also helps the group to learn to read well in unison.

The only thing I have found which the child cannot entirely appreciate and understand in the church service is the sermon. Most sermons are too profound for the junior age child. Some ministers feeling that they should speak to the children preach a short sermon for them at a designated place in the service. But a weekly diet of tiny sermonettes does not really appeal or have a place in an order of worship. I teach the children that the sermon is primarily for their parents, pointing out that if they listen closely they will find themselves gradually understanding more and more of what is being said. There are always some things they can understand if they are attentive.

Even though they understand nothing at all, if the choir is attentive they give other people in the church an opportunity to listen without being distracted. I remind the boys and girls, "Remember, we are in the front of the church where everybody can see us at all times during the service. If we are inattentive, it is conspicuous and distracting. So, even if we are not able to understand let us make the gesture of attentiveness. Sit very quietly and look at the minister."

Each fall we have a little confusion when new children come into the choir, because they come from the primary choir and have no experience in sitting quietly. We had one little boy who was very bright, but it was almost impossible for him to sit completely still. He looked around, twisted his head, and disturbed the other boys who sat near him. I found that he was also disturbing the older girls behind him and the adults farther back. So I asked two of my older boys, who were twelve, if they would object to my putting this child between them for a few Sundays, and maybe even permanently. I told them he was having a little trouble adjusting in church. I explained that I did not want to lose him from the choir, but that we could not have him disturbing others. I also pointed out that they always sat quietly and perhaps he would understand and follow their example. I told the young boy I knew he was having a problem in church and I could understand how that was because he was not used to sitting quietly. Perhaps the smaller boys around him were a little bothersome, so I was putting him with two of the big boys. He liked being with the older boys, partly because he was taller than most of the nine-year-olds and did not feel conspicuous with the larger youngsters. In two weeks there was quite a difference in him, and one of the boys told me proudly that he thought they had helped the child. He said, "I noticed one time he had his bulletin and hymnal at the wrong place, so I just put mine over a bit on my lap so he could see where I had mine. Another time he was playing with his book, so I just laid my hand on his and he stopped right away."

This solution was good for all my boys. It helped the older ones to feel the responsibility of setting an example for the younger boys, who in turn learn by experience and through admiration for the older boys. If this little boy sat with his parents in church I am quite certain he would still be wiggling and twisting because he would not get from them the same kind of pride in doing the right thing that he gets from the choir.

The boys and girls who sing every Sunday in church get very much attached to the idea of being there regularly and they do not want to miss a service. They are much stricter about this than the parents and often refuse to go on a trip over the week end if it involves missing the worship service.

In the summer we find that the choir members who have been regular all winter take their places with their parents and do exactly the things they have done during the winter in choir. They have the page ready for the responsive reading, stand at the right time for the hymns, and follow the choir rules regardless of whether the adults do so or not. So many people speak of how fine it is that the children are participating in the service. It is brought about through habit and practice.

Of course children do not fall into this pattern of fine behavior without training. They must be made to feel the importance of the choir on Sunday. It would help to give them something of the history of choirs to develop their understanding of the important place choirs have always held in the church. What is a choir? Why do we use them? What are the duties of a choir?

Membership in a choir means assuming certain obligations. It means being alert in any situation; it means being ready to do the right thing at the right time. A choir leads in worship, and no person can be a leader unless he always does his best. A leader has to do things correctly. A leader must be a little more alert than everybody else in order that he may set a good example. In a service a leader will have the hymn page ready, will be ready to stand at the right time, will be ready with the first word of the responsive reading. Always the choir member is ready. This readiness comes through constant work at rehearsal each week—putting time and energy into preparing ourselves so that we can lead. This must be instilled into the boys and girls, and the director must keep refreshing their memory.

If your minister is skillful in talking with children, he can help to present the idea of leadership. If he needs guidance you can talk over what you would like for him to say, but any minister will need to think through what the choirs mean in the service before he can talk with real meaning and sincerity to the children. His talk carries great weight, and an opportunity should be found to have him speak to them several times during the year.

I recall one minister who was particularly skillful in talking with children and who knew how to talk on their level. He would say something like this: "I just want to thank you for your help on Sunday mornings. It gives me such a good feeling when I come into the pulpit and see you in your place in church, for I know that you have prepared for the service and you are ready to lead. I know that I have prepared my part, and as I see us all there together, I think what a wonderful service this is going to be because all the leaders have prepared for it. It surely will say a great deal to other people. So I want to thank you for your work each week." Several times a year he would do this—never saying the same words but always conveying the idea that he depended upon them to help.

71

You know what that did to the children; they felt a tremendous sense of responsibility.

I have found that well-trained children will rise to any emergency. They always seem to keep their heads and to do whatever is necessary. Through a misunderstanding at a choir dedication service my boys were given instructions by a choir mother which were different from mine. They knew they were doing the wrong thing, but they did what they were told and did it well. It meant that the choir ended up in a bad location for getting out on the recessional hymn, but they took care of that problem themselves in fine style. They told me later they knew they were at the wrong place, but they could not check with me at the organ so they thought they should do what they were told. I agreed, because it might be that sometime I would have to send word of a change in plans. So I congratulated them for keeping their heads and getting out smoothly at the recessional. I also told them how many adults had complimented them on handling the problem so well, and this helped their feelings since they had really worried about doing something wrong.

Since we usually have only one anthem each Sunday, the boys and girls do not sing an anthem alone very frequently. However, we do use many anthems with the children and adults combined. Both groups stand at the same time, but the children do not turn to face the congregation. If they turned around they would be self-conscious standing so close to the congregation. It is also a temptation to start looking for friends and relatives. Furthermore, turning to face the congregation tends to put the children on parade and this should always be avoided. The choir members cannot see me and I cannot see them from the organ, and no one gives any cues. The music is worked and worked at the piano first with the introductions to their parts, and then we transfer to the organ for further preparation. There are a few anthems which have given me moments of panic when the accompaniment is tearing along with little clue as to where the children should begin, but so far they have never failed to come in correctly. To me this shows that they understand the importance of careful preparation. If the children are to sing they must look nice. That means they will need guidance in putting on vestments. This is the job of the Choir Mothers' Guild —to see that the vestments are in good condition, put on neatly and carefully, fastened properly, and that the collars are right. Hair must be combed and there must be no jewelry showing. The girls are to wear no hair ribbons, no colored socks. I have always wished that I could ask all to have black shoes but I feel that I cannot. Instead, it is dark shoes and white socks. I am positive that good appearance makes a difference to children in their attitude toward the service. When they feel they look right they have added confidence.

The choir mothers have the job of seeing that the children are in the right place at the right time and that they are quiet. A child cannot come out of church school, perhaps feeling a bit rambunctious because he is free to move about, get on a vestment and come tearing down to get in line for church and then be in the right attitude for worship. This creates one of the biggest jobs for the choir mothers. They must allow a little time for letting off steam but must know how far they can let the steam blow. Then they must know when to get the group calmed and quiet, ready to go into the sanctuary. The children must assemble their hymnals (which should be in good condition—not torn or ragged)—and the morning bulletin. A short prayer by the minister, the director of music, or one of the choir members puts the whole group into the proper mood for worship. After the service the mothers see that the children return robes and hymnals to their proper places.

I almost like to spend more time with these details than I do with singing, because I think it is of such importance that we train in worship at this age. It is a direct tie-in with the music they are learning—learning to worship; learning to sing worship music worshipfully.

Junior Choir Materials

WE HAVE TALKED ABOUT TUNES AND TEXTS WITH the primary choir, now we need to discuss music to be used with juniors. They can learn almost any interval, and rhythmic changes and difficult patterns do not bother the junior chorister as they do adults. A change in time signature is taken in stride by the children, while some adults panic when they see such a change.

The director must be very critical as he searches for song material for the choirs. The market is being flooded today with "pot-boilers" written to exploit the children's choir field, and no publisher's catalogue is without blemish. Sometimes pruning of a section of a song may solve the problem; again, the only solution is the wastebasket.

Many illustrations come to mind of inferior songs which children are taught to sing wholeheartedly and with fervor because some adult has introduced it to the child with enthusiasm. We must face up to the fact that this sort of thing cannot be continued, for the public schools are training youth to accept excellent things. For instance, what are the boys and girls in high school singing? Bach chorales, motets by Palestrina, cantatas, and oratorios. They are learning fine choral music, but when they come to church what do we expect them to sing? Something stuck back in the corner for years—something which some misguided person thought was good when he was a child but which has little or no appeal to youngsters nowadays.

Many of the songbooks which are used in various children's departments contain songs of decidedly inferior quality, and many which were all right in their day have no place in education today. It is not that we are merely teaching songs for the children to sing today only; we are teaching them music and texts which will stay with them a lifetime. Even if the songs are temporarily forgotten, they will bring back certain associations when heard again. The question is whether we have taught Christian truth in its best form and whether we have taught musical taste of lasting value. It behooves us to be careful in the selection of our material, choosing only those things which are worthwhile and significant.

Choose material which offers plenty of variety—in meter and in melodic patterns. A steady diet of 4/4 time becomes monotonous. Children need change, and they also like to dig into challenging music—music which offers some vocal difficulties. The vocal range can be increased at this age. Most children can be taught to sing up to *g, a* flat, and even *a* without too much trouble.

In our choices we must consider the text as well as the tune. This is true whether we are choosing a hymn, an anthem, or a song in a church-school worship book. Many times a good tune is ruined by a poor text, and of course the reverse is true. In regard to text, we want that which has literary value—good construction and beauty of thought and expression. It should certainly be something for which we need not apologize. The words should express religious verity. This does not mean that we sing nothing but religious songs in the rehearsal, for other material will be used. The texts, however, should have some bearing on religious matters and should teach Christian truths and the Christian way of life.

I do not do much with a second part in the junior choir, since it takes so much time to work out the second part that many other more important matters are sidetracked. So except for an occasional spot where there might be a division of notes into thirds or some simple harmony, we use unison music with the juniors. I do feel that they should begin to get the feel of parts, hence the use of rounds, canons, and descants. These help the children learn to hold one part against another.

Whatever the material you have chosen to teach, sing it over and over to yourself, thinking about how it should be sung and where the problems are. Take a phrase and sing it over three or four times, trying it in different ways. It takes time to find both good materials and the best presentation, and your decision about presentation must be made before rehearsal begins.

I have often been asked, "How do you keep the children interested in coming Sunday after Sunday when they almost never sing an anthem alone?" My only answer is that I try to emphasize the importance of leadership in worship more than simply singing anthems alone. I do not let them get the idea that they come only because they are singing something "special"—a word I dislike intensely when applied to church music. Music ought not to be special; it ought to be a part of worship every Sunday. If children are interested in the church service and their contribution to it, I do not believe they will be bothered about when they are to sing alone. I cannot remember, in all honesty, when my juniors have asked me when they are going to sing alone in church.

At the same time, many anthems intended for adult voices have a solo part which may be adjusted for use with children. Soprano, mezzo, or tenor solos are better for children's voices than alto or bass. The contrast of the light, delicate tone with the full four part harmony is very effective. One does not have to find anthems that are written especially for children and adults, for many can be adjusted to fit a graded choir presentation if the director uses a little imagination. Of course, care must be taken of the choice of texts.

One of the songs which we like to sing at Thanksgiving is "All Thy Works Praise Thee," arranged by Charlotte Lockwood Garden. The tune is called "Rock of Ages" in some hymnals. It is a Hebrew tune and lends itself to graded choir treatment. Although the first stanza is arranged in four part harmony, I have the children sing it in unison. The second stanza is sung by the adult altos, the third by the high-school girls, and all choirs join on the last. The tune is most singable, and the words are appropriate for children. This is just one example of many anthems which can be arranged to include the juniors.

I am always on the watch for anthems which can be sung antiphonally. Jungst's arrangement of "While by Our Sleeping Flock

We Lay" is good, with the children singing the echo "Joy, joy, joy." Other anthems which may be used by two or more choirs are listed in the Bibliography.

In addition to anthems, there are many other songs you should consider for the junior choir. Children enjoy singing spirituals, so have a collection handy. You will find collections of folk songs, fun songs, and rounds—such as those published by the Cooperative Recreation Service, in Delaware, Ohio—very useful. Rounds are excellent for teaching part singing and useful for relaxation. "Thirty-five Sacred Rounds and Canons" by Lee Hastings Bristol is full of short, attractive rounds. And while "Rounds and Canons" by Harry R. Wilson contains many more difficult canons, there are several pages of short, easy ones included.

The junior age is a time when we can begin to teach hymns very thoroughly, for juniors are capable of learning quickly and retaining what they learn. In selecting hymns, consider the following:

1. *Range.* Be careful to choose tunes which fit the children's voice range. If there is a low note, be sure the children do not force the voice down to it. The higher registers are safer at this age.

2. *Rhythm.* Choose hymns which are rhythmically attractive and whose rhythmic pattern underlines and strengthens the words.

3. *Words.* Are the words easily pronounced? Can they be understood by boys and girls of junior age? Are the words meaningful rather than fanciful? Are the theological expressions within the grasp of the children? It would, for instance, be almost impossible for children to understand the imagery of "There Is a Fountain Filled with Blood."

4. *Subject matter.* The subject matter must be understandable, but this does not mean that it cannot be slightly over their heads. Many a fine hymn may have some expressions of value which the

child can grow to understand. If the basic idea is clear, the complete picture will come into focus with the passing years. Subject matter is truly important, and at this point choir directors should consult with church-school leaders. The director should know what is being taught so that materials chosen for the choir are on a level with the lesson materials and are related to the basic theme. Get a set of the graded lesson plans and study them carefully; they will give an idea of the kind of texts to be chosen for singing and also the level of theological concepts being presented in the church school. You can secure these materials by asking the head of each department to provide them or by asking the church-school superintendent to order an extra set of all lesson materials for your use.

In working with hymns in the junior choir we have a chance to make a study of the hymnbook itself. Explain the different indexes —topical, first line, tune, composer, author. Show how to use the metrical index to find alternate tunes for hymn texts. A different index could be explained at each rehearsal. Very often if we have the hymnal open before us, I will ask one child the name of the tune, then ask if there are other sets of words to that same tune in the hymnbook. This is a good test of whether children really know how to use the book. Since we rehearse all of the hymns to be sung on Sunday, the choir has plenty of opportunity to find its way around the hymnal.

The children also need to know the main sections of the hymnal, usually shown in the Contents. They should be able to find the hymns of praise, then hymns for various seasons. Sometimes the topical index, rather than the Contents, has this information.

As you go through this study of the hymnal you can use various quizzes. Boys and girls of junior age are interested in tests of skill and quiz games. Mimeographed sheets of true-false questions or games matching tunes and texts are fun. You can play snatches of hymns for identification—a game which is not as easy as it would appear.

Materials will include many things, but the hymnal and its study is a major field of work which should not be neglected.

Vocal Training

CHAPTER VIII

AT THE JUNIOR AGE YOU CAN BEGIN TO DO SOME real training of the children's voices. During this age, and on into junior high groups, you will find the children imitating your vocal patterns. This calls for careful singing on the director's part and also careful instructions concerning the use of the voice.

During junior age the boys' voices tend to be more beautiful than the girls', and their tone is easier to blend and has excellent carrying quality. It is really no trick to get a group of children's voices to blend, although every director knows how difficult it is with adults. If the vowel is sung correctly the voices will blend because they are of approximately the same quality. It used to be said that the secret of training a child's voice was to have him sing softly. This is not a bad rule, but now we do not work for the pianissimo quality which was once sought after. Using the natural voice is the way to work at tone production.

Finding the natural voice is sometimes a problem. I recall one little boy who would sing out very loudly when I asked him to sing with his natural voice. He was actually forcing, but he thought this was his natural singing voice. I suspect that perhaps his parents had encouraged him to "sing out," or it is possible that he was trying to imitate someone he had heard on television or radio.

The child's natural voice is what we call a head tone—a light, floating, easily produced tone. No child should be allowed to develop a chest tone, for it is unnatural and results in depressing the voice box and forcing the tone. The voice should be kept "up." I have used this device for encouraging good production—I tell the choir that when they sing naturally and easily I can understand them from a distance, but when they try to sing loudly I cannot understand them as well. I often go into another room and ask the children to sing two different ways and let me judge which way I can hear best. The children like to be convinced of things themselves, and since juniors are questioning people, I sometimes send one of them out to listen.

Another helpful device is the use of mental pictures. I recall having difficulty with a summer group which was inclined not to focus the tone, so there was no carrying quality. I drew for them a mental picture of a street two blocks away, with a tree holding a nest and a bird. The bird could not leave the nest because there were eggs in it and yet the bird wanted to hear the choir sing. Did they think they could make the bird hear them? The first reaction was to sing very loudly. So I sent someone from the room and asked him to listen. The decision was that this was noise, not singing, and that the bird would not enjoy hearing that at all. So the group tried again, and I told them that sometimes the small pure tone carries best. They tried to get a mental picture of the tree and the bird and sang directly to that spot. The tone then began to have focus.

Devices and games will aid in solving such problems; scolding never does. Fussing at children merely causes discipline problems.

Posture has a great deal to do with good tone, and on a dreary, sluggish day work on posture can do wonders for the tone. A completely relaxed posture is not good for singing, so from the beginning I insist that we stand or sit like the big choir does on Sunday. Keep insisting on this, for the smaller children have not yet formed habits of good posture for singing. Do not wear the children out with harping on sitting up, but be sure when they are actually to produce a song that their posture is good. Remember, they will reflect your posture! If you keep at it through the years you will find that there are fewer problems when you get to the junior age, since the habit of good posture will have been formed.

A very useful round for teaching posture is the following sung to the tune of "Frère Jacques" with suitable motions:

> Perfect posture, perfect posture;
> Do not slump, do not slump.
> You must grow up handsome, you must grow up handsome;
> Hide that hump, hide that hump.

This is lots of fun, good exercise, and relaxation and makes the point of good posture. There are other posture songs which create a desire to sit and stand tall, and posters are also helpful. Over the years I have noticed that the children have learned to sit any way they please when we are finding pages or preparing for some activity, but when it is time to sing they get their backs away from the chairs and sit up automatically.

If the posture is right very little need be said about breathing. There may be an occasional time when there is a long phrase, but for the most part the material they will learn will be of fairly short phrases which can be sung easily. I have a little accordion that I use sometimes with boys and girls of junior age. It is broken, having been left over from a choir group a long time ago; it makes no sound whatsoever and is perfect for illustrating ribs out. I can explain that for a long phrase we need enough breath to last, and I illustrate with the accordion—out and in, slowly or fast. Just as the accordion goes in and out, so do our ribs when we breathe.

The place that I have found more necessary than any other for work on breathing is in the beginning of songs. Too often the children are not ready to sing the first note and try to gulp in air as they begin. It is a question of being prepared, of thinking what note is to be sung, and being ready to sing by taking the breath just before the note. With a full breath there are fewer problems with pitch.

Next is diction, and this is one of your biggest problems. In *The Successful Children's Choir*, Ruth Jacobs has a section on page 35 entitled "Diction in the Children's Choir" which should be studied carefully. If the diction is good and if the sounds are created properly, the voice responds and the pitch line will be good. But if the sounds are swallowed and unclear the voice will be muddy and confused sounding. The book *So to Speak* by Elizabeth von Hesse is an excellent one for study, as is *The Singer's Manual of English Diction* by Madeline Marshall.

First, train your own ear to hear sounds. Some people have acute hearing and can detect diction problems almost at once. There are others who do not hear sounds clearly and are not conscious of diction inaccuracies. Experiment with your own voice until you can produce any sound exactly as you expect it to be produced by the choir. This means studying vowels, consonants, and diphthongs.

Try singing "O" in several different ways. Imagine that you are hearing yourself. Ask how your throat feels when you sing it a certain way. Notice how you shape your mouth. Which gives the best feeeling and sound? Experiment with sounds yourself. Do not be content merely to read what someone has said on the subject. Remember that children are questioners. They want to know why. Be sure you can explain why.

If you are unsure of the pronunciation of a word in a song, go to the dictionary for the exact pronunciation. Be sure you are correct and then think of ways to get the children to produce it correctly. The sound "I" for instance can be practiced by singing the word "my" and having the children think of the letter "y" as having two sounds—the last of which is an "ee" which is not put on until the signal for release. Take the children individually, if necessary, to make clear what you want. Sometimes this is the way to work on the problem of one child without singling him out immediately. Just go down the row and have each child sing the vowel alone.

Watch for the endings of words. We are all lazy and prone to leave off the ending consonant or at best not to make enough of them. On the other hand the choir should not use the exaggerated hummed "m's" and "n's" which are the stock in trade of many radio choruses. Particularly troublesome is the "ing" ending of so many words. This must be exaggerated at first so the children become conscious of the problem. Pure vowels are never enough— the ending consonants must be present. The best approach is to ask the children to imitate the vowel sound that you give them.

Time spent going over isolated sounds tends to be time wasted. Choose your examples and problems from the text at hand by picking out the defective word and then the defective sound. For instance, take the word "little." How much emphasis do you give to the final "l" sound? Does the choir say "liddle," or do they say "lit-tle"? Every word is a matter of concern.

Another thing we want to work on is staccato and legato singing. This is done largely through vocal exercises. The idea of a ball bouncing—touching the floor and bouncing right off again is one good illustration for staccato. Or boys may like the idea of a ball hitting a bat. Illustrations from the familiar help to get the idea across. Staccato singing can be practiced on a single note then on moving scale patterns, five notes at first and then eight. For accuracy and precision I prefer to have the children practice without instrument so their ears become alert to correct pitch. I sometimes use my hand to give directions by pretending to bounce a ball on the floor and having them sing with the bounce. This is interspersed with the imagined accordion so they must be ready to hold any note on cue. They do not know when the last note is going to come, so they remain alert. It is a device for keeping interest and for practicing two different skills.

Next I practice arpeggios staccato. When the children are skillful at this I have them take one arpeggio up and down staccato followed by one legato. I also spend time on quick attacks and quick releases for alertness. Sometimes I give signals for these with my head instead of my hand so they can become used to watching for all kinds of cues.

Another device is the train whistle—"toot, toot, toot"—sung staccato. The "oo" sound is easy to produce and easy to pitch, while the "t" is good for consonant attack and release. We use this as if the train were picking up speed, moving faster and faster. This is done on hand signals and it calls for concentration.

Exercises can be made from any sound, any word which causes difficulty. If you know that in February you are to sing a song that has many slighted endings you should start games in the fall which will have the choir prepared to do these endings correctly when the time comes for its presentation. The choir does not need to know the reason behind the early start, but it will make your later work much easier. Try to think of original ways to present the sounds so that the same pattern is not used every time. It may tax your imagination, but interest will lag if you fail to make changes in presentation.

Clear diction and smooth legato demand that all singers pronounce all words exactly alike and in unison. Therefore you must spend considerable time teaching the children to form sounds and to connect these sounds simultaneously. Practice in moving together from vowel to vowel, connecting tones but forming each one distinctly, can be made into a game or contest. Later on, consonants and vowels should be alternated; spell out words and sing them on fixed or movable pitches.

I use the picture of a string of beads with each touching the other without overlapping. Each is a separate unit but it takes all of them evenly spaced to make a beautiful strand. I have actually used big beads on a string to illustrate this. I also divide the choir into small groups of two or three and let one group listen to see if they can tell when everybody is singing in unison, is producing the same vowel, and is singing a true legato. In this way the ear is trained along with the voice.

The "coo" sound is a good one for practice since the vowel is so easily produced. I also use "hoo" as a help in getting the vowel started, particularly in staccato singing. The "h" helps to get the push from the diaphragm. If there is a wide skip, such as an octave jump, the "h" in front of each note helps to make the pitches accurate. There is such a jump in the anthem "One Early Easter Morning," by Marryott, involving an upward jump from d to d on the words "one early." There is a tendency to tighten the throat on the upper pitch on the word "early," particularly when singing the passage softly. So we put an "h" in front so the word becomes "hearly." The "h" never comes through to the listener but it helps to get the throat open, which in turn helps to get the top note on pitch.

Other exercises can be constructed on the five note (c to g) pattern which is so widely used by voice teachers. These are done on different vowels, moving the scale pattern up and down by half steps. These should be done in combinations of legato and staccato.

There are several good books on voice and vocal exercises which should be helpful. You will also find it to your advantage to study privately with a good voice teacher. Be sure to ask the reasons for the exercises that you are given so you can use them intelligently with the children. The public school music teacher should be able to help you at this point of vocal pedagogy, and of course you will want to have many discussions with your fellow directors who are working at the same problems.

Since you will probably get your children after school, there are several particular vocal problems to watch for. The slumped position caused by weariness will cause children to sing just under pitch. Poor ventilation may be causing trouble, for a hot room is not good for singing. Breathing habits may be causing trouble, for correct breathing is the foundation of all good singing. Certain vowels may not be easy to sing on pitch, and any weariness will cause the children to give less attention to the problem. Sometimes flat singing may be caused by the failure of the child to get enough breath to sustain a long phrase. If consistently through a long period of rehearsals the children still sing a song slightly under pitch, try changing the key of the piece. A change of only a half step (either up or down) will often turn the trick.

When the children are to sing publicly there are apt to be some vocal problems caused by nervousness or self-consciousness. On some of the higher notes particularly there may not be sufficient breath to put the notes exactly on pitch. If you are conducting the children you can give added confidence by your manner and your gestures. A signal for deeper breathing before a high note or a long phrase, a finger pointed up to indicate a higher pitch, the hand indicating phrase contours—all these will do much to help the children gain needed confidence. If the children have to sing without direction, one big help is to find some spot on which their gaze is directed so they do not feel self-conscious about being looked at by the congregation—probably some spot slightly above the heads of the congregation at the rear of the church.

Many children develop a fear of notes that seem to go high in pitch, and this causes them either to flat the notes or to strain the voices trying to reach them. To forestall this I give indications sidewise rather than up and down. For instance, for an octave jump I start on my left and move the hand over to the right. The same method can be used in delineating arpeggios, with the hand bouncing sideways. It is a visual aid, but when accompanied with a good body position and proper breathing illustrated by the director it is amazing to see the difference this approach makes in the way the children sing the higher notes.

You will find that certain vowel sounds cause difficulty in pitch. If you do not know what they are, you will soon discover them when you try to sing a song that calls for certain words on high pitches. Some notes will sound flatter than others. If you examine carefully what is happening to the throat as you produce these vowels, you will find that the closed vowels have to be modified or opened to sustain the pitch. The open throat words will be on pitch if the posture is good and breath support right, but the squeezed sounds willl be pinched and off pitch.

One year in the Lynchburg Junior Choir Festival my choir was asked to sing a descant written by William Schutt to "O Beautiful for Spacious Skies." It opens with an octave jump from *g* above middle *c* to the *g* above on the words "O beau-(tiful)." The choir consistently had trouble with landing on the top note in tune. They came close, so we tried all sorts of tricks. The "u" sound was the problem, but trying to sing it with open throat was no solution. Finally I said, "Everybody else will be singing the words 'O beautiful,' but we will modify the vowel and sing 'O bootiful.'" The change was never noticed and the "oo" vowel was easy to produce. There was no more pitch problem after that.

Pitch assurance can also be worked on through rhythmic response. When the children understand, feel, and can interpret the rhythm of a song they are more apt to give a better pitch response also.

There is a twofold approach to the artistry of good interpretation. On one hand, interpretation comes with the understanding of what one is trying to do—the intellectual approach. We must understand the text, the idea, the mood, and the spirit of the song. We must understand what we are trying to convey to other people through the words and the accompanying music. The second approach is the physical, or rhythmic, response which children often feel instinctively. We have as much or more trouble with rhythm problems in adult choirs as with anything else, for adults have developed inhibitions which keep them from responding to the rhythmic patterns of music. But little children seem to respond instinctively to rhythm in that they move when they hear music. They may be waving their hands, running to quick music, or simply moving their bodies. As they grow older they stop making this physical response, perhaps because they do not see others doing it and become self-conscious. Unless we keep this response to rhythm going in choirs we lose one of the most important factors in the interpretation of music. You have heard choirs lose the rhythm by carrying over notes too long, stopping for breath in the wrong places, not being responsive to the flow of music.

Therefore, I think it is most important that we keep children doing rhythmic exercises in the choirs. It is not only good activity —it accomplishes much in terms of a better choir. This should include, with small children, songs and games imitating animals and sounds of nature. But we should go further and encourage them to work out imaginative, creative responses to music. In the book *Creative Rhythmic Movement for Children* by Gladys Andrews, there are many suggestions for various movements. You should "realize that the way of starting rhythmic responses is unimportant. The essential element is to get started. How one approaches a group, what one starts with, depends on what one knows about children, their needs, varying stages of development, interests, and former experiences." This book suggests many questions and procedures for starting.

It is at this point of body response that I like to do more serious work with interpreting the music we are singing. Here is an opportunity to get children to think more deeply about the text—combining the intellectual and the physical approach. Take a hymn or carol (these are particularly good) that the children know and ask them what they can do in the way of movement with the words of the hymn. How can we interpret it with our bodies? Gradually children will develop a good bit of originality in response as they go through the hymns. As the words move the body responds in such a way that there is no stopping of the rhythmic flow of words or music.

"For the Beauty of the Earth" is a hymn with which I usually start because it is easy and familiar. We begin by talking about the beauties of the world about us, depending on the season of the year, then talk of our thanks to God who has given us all these beautiful things—"Lord of all, to Thee we raise this our hymn of grateful praise."

Then we take the first phrase, "For the beauty of the earth," and see how we can express this with our bodies. Almost at once the children who have never done this sort of thing before will point to the earth. So I always say, "Yes, that is a possibility, but if we point to the earth we point to just one spot and I think the song intends to be all the earth." Soon they get the idea of giving an outspread motion, not necessarily fast, since the song does not suggest great speed. If they want to look in both directions or all around this may help to express the magnitude of the earth.

"For the glory of the skies" calls for an upswept motion. "For the love which from our birth" is rather more difficult for most children. Generally we end by thinking in terms of how each one of us is surrounded by love. In every place there are people who love us—our parents, our friends. Everybody is surrounded by love and over us all is the great love that God has for every person. So we end by bringing down the gesture to embrace space around us and then to ourselves.

We have indicated only the first three phrases, but we have created continuous movement so the child is not resting at all. As the music goes forward he is moving in interpretation. On the last line "Lord of all, . . ." I get a variety of reactions. No group of children ever suggests the same interpretation. One group said they

93

thought this was a prayer in which they were speaking to God. They felt they wanted to kneel, so they knelt and held out their hands as they sang the last phrase. Other groups have thought of it as being an offering so they merely lifted up their hands in an offering gesture.

It is better to suggest ideas to children than to tell them what to do. By suggesting that the song is floating out over the skies the movements can become flowing and continuous without awkward breaks. This of course is a more restricted form of movement than the free movement used with small children playing they are horses or elephants or marching in rhythm to music. But the text of a hymn so interpreted does take on added meaning which is not easily forgotten. The symbolic movement has helped to give a more artistic interpretation and a more complete understanding of the text.

"All Creatures of Our God and King" is a good hymn for interpretation and the "Alleluias" offer many possibilities for treatment. Of course hymns with a marching rhythm offer the double possibility of combining movements with a marching pattern.

Margaret Fisk, in her book "The Art of the Rhythmic Choir," suggests that "In Christ There Is No East or West" can be done in the following manner: The group forms a circle and numbers off "ones and twos." Then the group joins hands for the first stanza:

> In Christ there is no East or West,
> In Him no South or North;
> But one great fellowship of love
> Throughout the whole wide earth.

The group simply moves around "the whole earth," walking in a circle with hands joined. Then the ones and twos face each other in pairs for the next stanza, which is the third stanza in the hymnals. They then do, in square dance parlance, a Grand Right and Left to the words:

> Join hands, then, brothers of the faith,
> Whate'er your race may be.[1]

This suggests the picture of joining hands with all the brothers and sisters of the world as the circle illustrating the earth is continued in another form. On the last stanza the ones simply step out away from the twos, and step inside to form an inner circle. They join hands and lift their arms up high. Then the twos from the outer circle join hands and on the last line of the hymn the outside circle comes under the arms of the inside circle, the arms of the inner circle now around the backs of the others and the group is now one big earth, all joined together in love.

The director's job is to get the children to think of interpretations. It matters not if their pattern is different from the one you have thought out; it is better to allow each child to work out his own interpretation if he wishes. If some want to kneel to illustrate a phrase in a hymn, fine; but perhaps others do not feel this is the right interpretation. The creative urge should be nurtured instead of submerged.

In developing rhythmic response I have found folk games very useful. I am fortunate in having a chorister whose father is a specialist in this field and from time to time we have parties where he teaches some of the folk games. In most of these games there must be a definite pattern rather than a free response, but it does encourage the rhythmic response to music.

---

[1] Words from *Bees in Amber* by John Oxenham. Used by permission.

If work in rhythm is started with the very small child and continued with the juniors, the junior high age group will want to extend it to their group.

The book by Gladys Andrews also has a chapter on percussion instruments and movement. We have tried tapping on the chairs and on the floor with the hand, the foot, or small sticks. Then I have asked the children, "How does this kind of rhythm make you want to move?" Often a low thumping sound reminds the children of elephants, but other sounds bring other physical movements and reactions. The book also offers ideas for using easily available materials to create percussive instruments.

Of course you will continue with note reading and theory. Spend time learning how to build all kinds of scales—major, minor, whole tone, chromatic, modal, pentatonic—and translating them into vocal patterns. This involves learning why there are different intervals and recognizing various scale patterns. Singing by the do-re-mi's (syllables) is fun and can be taught in small doses from time to time with the hymnal as a ready resource book of reading material.

Conducting is another subject that juniors enjoy. They are able to follow definite patterns for various time signatures, and they should be trained in conducting. Give them all of the simple patterns of conducting—3/4, 4/4, and 2/4 time. Later add 6/8 which is a bit more complicated. Let them all beat time while you play. Let each child conduct the rest of the choir.

Juniors are old enough to begin to approach music on its own level, for its own sake. It is no longer a game with them. Much in the music will be attractive because of the musical design, and time should be spent analyzing the music learned. It is at this age that much can be done to establish a fine taste for excellent music.

The Junior-High Choir

 THE JUNIOR-HIGH AGE PROBABLY OFFERS MORE difficult problems, both vocal and psychological, to the director than any other age group. First of all, let us look at some of these problems and then some suggestions for solution. Adolescent boys and girls have little or no confidence in their singing. They have little voice to sing with and they are embarrassed because they cannot seem to do better. This age may cause you disappointment occasionally when they sing in church. I have had groups which sang beautifully in rehearsal but poorly in church services, when their voices thinned out because of self-consciousness.

Nevertheless it is very important to keep this choir active, and one of the best ways to do this is to assign regular times for the junior-high choir to be responsible for music leadership in the services. Where a church has double services this choir can share responsibility for one of the services. If they have some particular objective they are more likely to stay with the church at a time when many young people are dropping out.

At this age most boys and girls will come to choir only if they feel it is worth their while, and this presents a real challenge to the director. It is easy to become discouraged with their progress, yet the choir can be a stabilizing influence on them during a particularly difficult time. Junior-high youngsters seem to be in need of special attention, and the choir director is in a good position to see that there are opportunities for them to feel needed and important. Honors granted by church and school must be noted, birthdays remembered, and graduations observed with a greeting card or telegram. A bulletin board with newspaper clippings about choir members, pictures of the group, and notices about coming events is useful. A real bond of Christian fellowship may be developed through service to other groups in the church. Setting tables for family night suppers, singing in old people's homes, baking cookies for a meeting of the auxiliary, making place cards and decorations for choir dinners—all of these and many more activities will help to emphasize the necessary "togetherness" of the group.

This age group enjoys music which has mood to it, and they also enjoy formal music such as the Bach chorales. They like fanciful music, for their tastes are as extreme as their moods. You must also remember that although they may seem indifferent, they enjoy singing, and it is wise to provide opportunities for them to do so.

Many of our Lynchburg junior-high boys and girls missed the junior choir festival which we hold annually, so as they moved on to the older group we organized a *Gymanfa Ganu* (Welsh hymn sing) to meet their need. This was made a city-wide activity, including both junior-high and high-school choirs, and it held the boys and girls together with a mutual goal and interest.

Discipline is a major problem at this age, and the director must be firm yet considerate. It is a particularly trying time for the girls; they are shy and self-conscious and embarrassed about their voice inadequacies. They do not know what they want to do nor why they want to do it. They can be completely unpredictable and certainly do not want to be told anything. I remember that once on two successive Sundays I received reports that two of my junior-high girls were holding a buzz session during the church service and annoying people nearby. At the next rehearsal I said something like this: "You know I am very fond of you, and we have worked together for many years, but I must tell you that sometimes you annoy and irritate me. I have a great deal of sympathy for you during a difficult time, and I think I can understand why you do certain things. I suppose if you do not hurt anybody when you are that way, it does not matter, but often there are other people involved who can be hurt, bothered, or annoyed. What we do in church at eleven o'clock on Sunday morning is something that concerns everybody in the church, not just you." That was all I said, but they knew perfectly well what I meant, and there has been no trouble since.

I have lost my temper with both boys and girls occasionally, but this only makes me feel bad afterwards and merely antagonizes them. When I am kind but firm the reactions are always better. I believe one of the best things we can do for them is to help them meet their problems individually and collectively. If I seem to have

99

departed from music and singing in speaking of this age group, it is because I feel that it is at the point of personal relations that a choir director will best reach these youngsters and will be able to accomplish something constructive. The director must know them, try to understand them, constantly read books and articles about them, and observe them in all situations for clues to their thinking and behavior. Remember that what they do and what they feel are often two different things.

Probably much of the problem with boys at this age lies in the area of voice change and the resulting vocal difficulties. Most of the boys are maturing more slowly than the girls, and in churches where there is a separate choir for boys the problem is partly solved for a portion of the junior-high period.

What to do with the boy's changing voice is an unsettled question, and there are many contradictory ideas. Some voice teachers insist that the boys should continue to sing during voice change. Others say that the boys should not sing at all during this period, particularly if it involves falsetto singing. Many graded choir programs plan acolyte guilds, handbell choirs, and similar activities for the boys during the period of voice change. Irving Cooper, in his books *The Singing Teens* and *Tune Time for Teen Time,* has arranged a great deal of music for this particular voice stage which he calls *cambiata*—music written in an extremely small range to make use of the notes still in the voice. *Cambiata* music may be the answer; having a boys choir of mixed voices may be the answer; or there may be some other solution which you will find for your church. It is a question as to what the director feels is best, and every individual must solve the problem in his own particular situation. Needless to say, the voice should be handled carefully during this period, and the wise director will do a great deal of study on the subject.

100

Strangely enough girls' voices change also, although not to the degree that boys' do. The change is not as obvious, and many people do not realize that girls may be having vocal difficulty all through high school. Each individual varies, but the girl of about twelve to fourteen has a breathy voice—breath completely surrounding the tone. It has lost its power as it changes from the child's voice to the woman's voice. The voice may remain soprano but with a different quality. Some may keep a light floating quality, but others will find their tones deeper in quality if not in pitch.

At this age many girls have grown long, lanky, and thinner and do not have good support for tone. If they try to put any volume into the voice, they are likely to force very badly. The voice will be reedy sounding and less pleasant to the ear. The director should be on guard for correct breathing and should avoid trying to coax too much volume from the choir. The director should also be on the watch for signs of vocal strain induced by imitating popular singers of the torch variety. I was once asked to listen to a young girl who did a great deal of public singing around her home community. Her parents wanted me to advise whether or not she should take voice lessons. When she started singing I nearly fell off the piano bench. She was an exact imitation of a popular radio star, sliding, slurring, and forcing her voice until the muscles of her neck were sticking out. I hated to hurt the child or the parents, but I had to tell them that if she did not stop singing like that at once she would no be able to sing at all in a few years. I learned that there was no public school music program to guide her, and the song leader of the church school encouraged the group to sing loudly all the time, using this girl as an example of good singing!

Many girls' voices are neither soprano nor alto at this stage, although there are always exceptions—those who mature early and whose voices settle correspondingly. However, many may want to sing alto because they are afraid of singing high. The range of music chosen should never be real alto; a medium range is safest. Real alto quality is seldom found at this age, and care must be taken not to force the voices in the lower part too low. Plenty of vocalization will help to extend the range, and work on diction, breathing, and other vocal problems will help to build confidence and a sure foundation for later choir work. The choir rehearsals can almost be voice lessons, and the girls will enjoy being treated like adults at this point (on other days they will act like children). But above all, remember that their voices cannot stand the long, taxing, driving work that an adult can take.

If you should have a group that does not want to sing alto or second soprano all the time, it is well to divide the choir into two groups which will alternate in singing the high and low part. This involves choosing music which is really written for first and second soprano rather than soprano and alto. If boys and girls are singing together in this choir the boys will likely still be singing soprano and/or alto. Anthems which have alternate parts sung by boys and then by girls, canons, and unison anthems with descant will all be acceptable and not too difficult to perfect. Range is important, and the text should be chosen to appeal to the boys who, though they may still sing soprano, will not want to sing lullabies and such.

Vocal training with this choir will continue along the same lines as with the junior choir. Breathing exercises will be added and longer and more intricate vocal exercises may be used. Further, this age is ready to sing in two parts. Three-part work may be stimulating to this group, but material must be chosen which avoids extremes of high or low pitch.

You will already have done some work in the junior choir with canons, rounds, descants, and occasional divided phrases. These are all excellent preparation for part singing, but now the children must be taught one further and very important step. They must learn to listen to other parts, in order to blend tone, rather than to simply close their ears and stay on their own part. Again, as in developing all other musical skills, listening should be stressed. Harmonic endings may have been used occasionally with younger groups, but the junior-high-age child is by virtue of more experience and preparation more able to hear the second part and to sing it more musically.

When beginning two-part singing, it is wise to select anthems which have simple melody lines for each part and which have no intricate rhythmic patterns. Thus each group will be free to concentrate on its own part in relation to the other part. Many anthems are arranged with one section in unison, one in two parts, and one in unison with descant. This provides variety, and less rehearsal time is needed on a single number.

Most junior-high choirs develop out of a graded choir program which has trained younger choirs; but if you need to start one from the beginning, some of these suggestions may be helpful: (1) Have a party! Start as a social group and branch out by finding those interested. (2) Make friends with the group by expressing a sincere interest in them. (3) Let them do the inviting of members and the building up of the choir. If they are interested and proud of the choir, they will want others to join. (4) Elect officers in your choir and give them definite responsibilities. I know of one group which decided they wanted to have choir dues and elected a treasurer who kept careful records. They used the money to buy flowers for the altar, to have a picnic, to hold an ice cream party, and to send flowers to sick persons. The group had pride in their own organization and made their own rules.

The most natural means of getting interest in the choir is through the youth fellowship group of the church. The director should meet with them and help with group singing, attempting to get en-

103

thusiasm for singing which can be carried over into developing a choir. If there is an opportunity to help with the music in the church-school class this may be a means of arousing interest in a choir, but the informal atmosphere of a fellowship meeting is more conducive to good results.

The Rehearsal

CHAPTER X

IDEALLY THE CHURCH SHOULD PROVIDE A SEPA-
rate room to be used by the choirs, but in many
places the space problems are such that this is
impossible. If there can be such a room it can hold
all equipment and be made attractive with posters and pictures. If
you must use several rooms it is usually best to have the various
choirs meet in their own church department rooms—that is, the
primary choir in the primary room, the juniors in the junior room.
In this arrangement the chairs and equipment are geared to the size

of the children and there is a feeling of being at home and at ease. A small child does not feel comfortable on a big chair, and if his feet are dangling for a long period of time he becomes tired and restlesss.

Whatever room you have, use it consistently. Shifting from room to room is demoralizing to a choir group, so make sure the rehearsal room is scheduled for the entire season. If an outside group wishes to use the space at the choir's regular time, let the outside group make the adjustment, not the choir.

The room should be of adequate size to hold the choir comfortably without crowding and should have good acoustics with no major problems of echoes or deadness. It should have plenty of light—natural light preferably, but with good lighting fixtures for dark days. There should also be good ventilation with windows which can be opened at the top to allow complete circulation of air. A room can be freshened rapidly by opening a few windows at the top to allow the stale air to rush out without sending in wintry blasts on the children's feet. Ventilation is a major concern, for singing calls for deep breathing and a consequent large turnover of air. A stuffy, hot room is ideal for sleepiness but not for singing, and since most rehearsals are held in the afternoon there is a tendency for the children to be sluggish anyway. The room should be attractive in its color scheme and decoration, avoiding all dullness. Some kind of growing flowers or plants will add cheerfulness, as will cut flowers in season.

The room should contain a bulletin board and a blackboard. If there are two bulletin boards one can be used for pictures and items of interest and the other for notices, announcements, rules, and other choir information.

Rehearsals are hard on music. Music is an expensive item in the church budget, and care must be taken to make it last as long as possible. Often each choir elects its own librarian, and this child is reponsible for the distribution, collection, and necessary repairing of music. There must be regular shelf space or a cabinet for storing music, and if certain music is the property of one choir only, the name of that choir should be stamped on the covers. You will find that children who are carefully trained in the handling of a hymnal will automatically have regard for anthem books or octavo scores.

Perhaps a few more words are needed on the subject of chairs. If the room does not have the right size chairs for children, arrangements should be made for the janitor to set up proper equipment before the rehearsal. It is better not to have the young children do this, for the activity of moving a lot of chairs can get a group excited, with confusion resulting. With older children perhaps helping with the chairs may be a means of working off steam, and most junior-age children wish to be called on for help.

The room should, however, be in readiness when the children arrive. The rehearsal can be difficult if they see you dashing around in a last minute flurry, for they sense a lack of quietness and readiness. The director needs to be present long before rehearsal time to see that the room is attractive, chairs are in place, music ready. When the children come you will have time to spend with them, talking and listening. If everything is ready there will be fewer discipline problems, for if you stop to look for something in the middle of rehearsal you invite trouble.

When a director has another job which does not allow her to be present for any great length of time before the rehearsal, or when the director has several rehearsals in one afternoon, one of the members of the Choir Mothers' Guild should take over the responsibility of being present to meet the children, perhaps having a story hour or a game period. Some churches with fine recreational facilities plan a period of activities before or after the choir, making a well-rounded program for the afternoon. If it is possible for the children to assemble somewhere other than the choir rehearsal room they are more in the mood for work and rehearsing if they come into the rehearsal room only in time to sing. When the children arrive early and use the choir room for playing, drawing on the board, and playing "chopsticks" on the piano it is difficult to get the rehearsal under way successfully. If someone other than the director can handle this period the work is aided greatly.

It is important that each child feel there is a special greeting for him. The timid child will not come to you, so you should make a special effort to let him know he has been noticed. You do not necessarily have to speak to each child in turn and call his name, but you should try to look at each child and acknowledge his presence in some small way. If there is any reason for saying something special to any child, mention this before rehearsal. Comment on a new baby in the home, a special school event, his piano lessons, whether his father is back home from a trip, or that you saw his name in the paper. Comments concerning clothes, however, are not wise, for this can set up jealousies. Make each child feel that he is an important chorister and is needed and loved.

During rehearsals keep a cheerful attitude, for children respond to this more quickly than they do to fussing. This does not mean that you will not be firm, but combine firmness with kindness and enthusiasm. Children will mirror your mood and attitude, and if you look forward to rehearsals, so will they. If you act confused or disturbed the children will be hard to manage because they will sense your anxiety. If you feel nervous or angry, stop and breathe deeply before you speak or act—it will help you to become calm. There will be many days when you will not feel like being enthusiastic, but you must learn to control your emotions in the rehearsal at all times.

108

At the first rehearsal of the year explain to the choir what rules and regulations are to be followed during the year. Make them brief, easy to understand, and fair. Be sure the children understand them. Have these printed in some form so the parents can be handed a copy. Do not make the rules so involved that no one pays attention to them or can follow them. Also at the first rehearsal explain any procedures which you plan to use—such as taking the roll. Some choirs have the children take a tab with their name off a hook to indicate their presence. Others call the roll with the children answering a sung phrase. Explain the need for being punctual and for staying to the end of the rehearsal.

Plan the rehearsal to move quickly, for variety is a must for a good rehearsal. Move rapidly from one thing to another so there is no time for the children to get out of the mood of rehearsal. There will be hymns to sing, new anthems to begin, old anthems to review, responses to learn, action songs, rhythm studies with clapping or marching, and other rhythmic interpretation. There will be exercises for tone and for breathing. There will be stories about the music or composers. Sometimes a nonsense song or round is good for breaking tension. There must be dozens of different approaches prepared for every rehearsal so that tiredness and boredom are avoided.

The director must learn to sense the feelings of the children and to guide them into different moods as the rehearsal progresses. This is sometimes very difficult. Particularly at Christmas time are the children keyed up and excited, and it is difficult to get them to work as efficiently as you wish. Therefore you should plan your work so that you begin the Christmas music well in advance; then it need only be reviewed and freshened up at the last few rehearsals.

An occasional visitor to the choir is good for the children. The minister should make an effort to attend occasional rehearsals. He can talk to the choirs about the importance of what they are doing, or perhaps he can explain how the music will fit into the service when they sing. Sometimes he may just come and sit for a little while without saying anything. You can prearrange a signal which indicates that he would like to say a few words and a convenient place in the rehearsal time can be made for his remarks. The children should feel that the minister thinks the choir is important enough for him to make time to visit.

It also helps to have some parents visit from time to time, for they catch the enthusiasm of the group, and it is good for them to see the work of the director and children. Members of the music committee should be invited to attend. If there are suggestions to be made for improvement in the program the members should know firsthand what is happening instead of getting information second-hand. You should also be willing to have choir directors from other churches visit your rehearsals.

If discipline problems arise during the rehearsal talk to the offenders privately after choir, if you can avoid interrupting the rehearsal at the moment of the offense. If a child is misbehaving, extra attention is called to the fact by stopping to scold—the children already know that he is misbehaving. If you appear un-ruffled, the choir probably will not take too much notice. If the problem recurs often, keep the child after rehearsal to find out the reason for the misbehavior. This can usually be done by merely talking with the child and asking what is bothering him. "Is it the music he does not like? Did something happen at school that upset him?" This personal attention is better than disrupting a rehearsal to solve the problem. It is particularly more effective in keeping the confidence of the children and letting them know that you are concerned with their personal problems.

To keep children interested for the year, plan your work with definite objectives. Children like something tangible to look forward to—a Thanksgiving service, a trip to a museum, a concert. Perhaps it is the Christmas vesper or the family choir night. Work far enough in advance so the children feel adequately prepared when they sing and can do their work confidently. Plan some diversions—trips, or parties with milk and cookies after rehearsal. Do not let choir become humdrum. Keep it an exciting experience.

Supplementary Materials

CHAPTER **XI**

 THERE IS MUCH MORE TO A CHOIR PROGRAM THAN walking into the rehearsal room and going through music with a group of children. A good choir rehearsal is the result of days and weeks of preparation. The director needs to work constantly to gather materials which will be helpful in keeping the rehearsal vital and alive.

In the matter of music, more is involved than finding good anthems. The progressive director will secure hymnals of all denominations and study them for usable material. For example, the

Presbyterian Church, U.S.A., has a series of fine hymnals for all ages. The Moravian Church also has a fine hymnal, and the Unitarian youth hymnal contains much material not found in other books. Of course the doctrinal side of hymns must be carefully studied to see if it is in conflict with your own church's beliefs. The director should also collect books which give information concerning hymns. This will mean the purchase of handbooks to various denominational hymnals plus books which will give additional and more detailed information about hymns and hymn singing.

Collections of descants will also be useful. As an introduction to part singing they are valuable, particularly with junior boys and girls. Descants can be used with combined choirs or with the entire congregation—provided the congregation is forewarned and does not stop singing during the hymn to listen to the children, and provided the descant is not used too frequently either in the service or with any one hymn.

A collection of pictures helps to illustrate hymns and anthems. Pictures from the church-school library will be especially helpful, but you will find many others on posters and in magazines. The younger choirs will enjoy bringing pictures to illustrate the songs they are learning. Magazines which are good resources are *Good Housekeeping, Woman's Day, Life,* and *Time*—to name only a few. Many of these pictures will be of children engaging in various activities. Mounted on construction or poster paper, they are beautiful and attractive decorations as well as good teaching material. Keep your eyes open as you read and you will find pictures of children, choir groups, stained glass windows, and dozens of other interesting subjects.

It is particularly helpful in developing interest in a boys' choir to use pictures of other boys' groups. One of the hardest jobs for a director is keeping the interest of boys, who are often afraid that

113

singing is sissy. If a choir of boys is touring your area, be sure to use pictures of the group. If you are publicizing a choir event, use pictures of boys if possible, for the girls do not seem to mind and it does give added prestige to the boys.

Your picture collection should also include pictures of composers. When you sing a number by a great musician, tell something about him and show his picture. Collect pictures of musical instruments. *The American Organist* publishes many beautiful prints of organs and organ cases. Music stores carry packets of pictures of various orchestral instruments, and you can secure large charts which show the various instruments and list their pitch ranges. The children can learn the different families of instruments and are given added encouragement to learn to play an instrument. Pictures of musical scores and musical notation, particularly examples of Gregorian chant, are always interesting to children.

Choirs like to see pictures of themselves, and it is good to keep a picture history of your choirs. These pictures may be snapshots or they may be taken by a professional photographer. In some churches a member of the congregation takes movies of the choirs each year and shows them at one of the choir parties. Colored slides can also be made and shown by projectors. The walls of the choir room at Memorial Methodist Church in Lynchburg are covered with pictures of choirs going back over eighteen years, and the children like to find brothers and sisters and even parents in older pictures. Pictures of your choir are useful for publicity.

I have found that juniors like to have notebooks or workbooks. Subjects for study could be Christian symbolism, famous church composers, the Christian year, religious art and architecture, stained glass windows, and similar topics. The church-school curriculum may suggest some themes, but the ideas should be related to the church and choir. This will no doubt lead you into some areas which will broaden your viewpoint and make you a better leader. You will find yourself studying various types of architecture in order to better present your own church building. You will be studying windows and symbols so you can explain them to the children.

A workbook project is a marvelous way to stimulate interest and to teach things the children may not learn any other place. A season spent in studying the Christian year is most worth while, for few churches give enough attention to this. If you have beautiful stained glass windows in your church you can plan a whole project around them. If a visit to a glass factory is not possible, many books on the making of stained glass are available from the library, and manufacturer's advertising brochures provide much information. The history of your church would make an interesting study, especially if the church is very old and has had many interesting events in its past. An especially rewarding project is a study of worship and worship patterns. *One God,* by Florence Mary Fitch, has beautiful illustrations showing Protestant, Catholic, and Jewish people at worship. This book has been put on film and is available from your denominational bookstore.

Posters can also be used successfully for teaching. From the pen of Mary Elizabeth Montgomery has come a fascinating series of posters on choir attitudes, processing, holding music, and similar subjects. These are available through the Music Department of Highland Park Methodist Church, Dallas, Texas. A series of such posters may help solve some of the problems in your choir.

As a choir director you will also build a record library, not only for use with the children but for your own development and musical training. Instrumental and orchestral works of short duration will find a useful place in your program as will great sacred choral masterpieces. It is unfortunate that there are so few recordings available of children singing children's songs. These are usually made by adults and ofttimes the vocal production is not what your children should imitate. There are, of course, recordings by choirs of boys such as the Vienna Boy Choir, the Columbus Boy Choir, and the Royal School in London. Some of these are most excellent, but we need to remember that the European approach toward the boy's voice is not always applicable to our choirs.

Recordings of organ music are also most useful, and it is now possible to buy LPs with several bands of shorter organ works. The King of Instruments series by the Aeolian-Skinner Organ Company is particularly effective, and the first record in the series is an interesting excursion into organ tone with illustrations of various organ stop sounds.

If the adult choir is presenting a major oratorio or cantata it is well worth the time spent to let the children hear portions of these works on recordings. For instance, children would be interested in hearing a recording of Haydn's *Creation* with its use of imitative orchestral effects. Since the work will probably be given in church with organ accompaniment the recording will broaden their concept of the intentions of the composer. If the children are learning one of the solos from *The Messiah* a good recording will help teach them and will be a guide to interpretation. This does not end the types and varieties of recordings which are useful, and the good director will be on the watch for fine recordings of all kinds.

Of course the choir director will collect books. Books of games and fun books may fill just the need for a moment of relaxation in the middle of a hard rehearsal. Party games for the social gatherings, rhythm games, action games, folk games—these are just a few of the needs which can be met with a good library.

Fun songs are always useful and such books as *Come, Let Us Be Joyful* and similar publications of the Cooperative Recreation Service should be on your shelf.

116

Books related to the church arts should be included in your collection, for you should deal with all of the arts, not music alone. Information about various kinds of architecture with pictures of churches all over the world will come in handy. Another art to be studied is wood carving. Many churches have examples either in the altar, chancel rail, or elsewhere. The First Methodist Church in Evanston, Illinois, has a particularly outstanding reredos with scenes from the life of Christ carved out of white oak. Many of the English cathedrals also have interesting carvings in connection with the organ case or choir stalls.

Reference works on church symbolism are an absolute must. Every church has some symbolic carvings, drawings, or windows, and the study of these can be a fascinating experience. Related to this field more extensively are books on worship. As director you need to know what is being done with various age levels in worship, and you should ask for suggestions and help from the church-school superintendent and church-school teachers. You will collect orders of worship from other churches, and from these you will receive ideas for building worshipful services. It is helpful to exchange church bulletins with many other churches, and most church musicians will be happy to arrange this at no charge, although in some cases there may be a small fee to cover postage. You will find yourself eternally indebted to others for the ideas you receive.

You will also keep a file of newspaper and magazine clippings— anything that may be useful. If the file begins to bulge you can always throw away material, but do not miss a chance to add something that looks interesting. A word of warning, however—have some system to your filing so you can find the article you want!

The choir program will be enriched by the acquisition of rhythm instruments for use with all the choirs, but more likely with the younger children. Many such instruments can be made from sticks, gourds, large spikes, pots, and pans.

Of course you will build a file of music—anthems, songs, collections—music of all sorts. Perhaps less has to be said about this than other materials since most choir directors do collect music. But do not be satisfied that you have everything. Keep on the watch for good new music.

Vestments

CHAPTER XII

ARE VESTMENTS NECESSARY FOR A CHOIR PRO-
gram? Definitely yes. In the first place they make
for a unified appearance which adds dignity to the
group. They also make each person appear the same
regardless of status in life. Vestments indicate a ministerial responsibility in the church; therefore they call for careful treatment.
Too often little attention is paid to the proper use of vestments, and
one finds them carelessly thrown on a hanger or dropped on the
floor in a heap. Choirs need to know that the vestment is a badge

of service they wear as servants of the church. They need to recognize that the church owns the vestment and that it is on loan to them, to be returned at the end of the season in good condition.

Many children at home are allowed to take off clothes and drop them anywhere without being required to hang up or pick up anything. On this point the director must be firm and establish good habits in the choir by playing up the importance and significance of the proper use and care of the vestments. This involves making it clear that once the vestment is put on the child's manner must become changed—there must be no running or playing. Tugging at one another pulls the garment out of shape and makes the choir look untidy, and such an attitude and appearance is not conducive to helping others worship. After the services the children should be trained to place their vestments in the proper place, not depending upon someone else to do this for them. If there is a definite place, and there should be, for a robe and hymnal, the child should be taught to place them correctly after the service.

There are all kinds of vestments, and your own denominational house will undoubtedly carry a wide selection. The choice depends on many factors. Some churches lend themselves easily to colored vestments for children, and most children prefer colors, as do most adults. However, there are some churches where the people feel strongly about anything other than black and white, and you should consider this before making a choice.

If you can eliminate the use of two piece vestments your work will be lighter. A one piece garment is easier to take care of, easier to put on and take off, and generally easier to clean. If you use black robes you must have something white on top of it, for black is too drab for use alone. A yoke of some kind is needed, and this can be in the shape of a cross, or round, or square. Of course the traditional form is the white cotta. At a junior choir festival in

Boston several years ago I saw more kinds of yoke sets than I had ever seen any place else, and all of them were quite effective. There were, however, many which were not on straight, and this is one of the problems with the double piece set. Unless the neck is small it is hard to keep the cottas on straight, and they must be pinned on the shoulders of each child each Sunday or else fitted very closely each year. A collar on a colored robe always looks neat and does not require special attention on Sunday. Before you buy, consider both the esthetic and practical sides.

If you use white collars (or the white cottas) there will be laundry expense to be included in your budget. If the children are giving their service to the church, the church should be responsible for the expense of the upkeep of robes and collars. If each person takes the collar home to launder you will get an uneven appearance since some persons will use more starch than others. There are many kinds of collars, each requiring different handling, but you should consider the upkeep when you make your choice. There is now a cotta of a silk-like texture which does not need to be starched and hangs freely and gracefully. It also does not show soil easily.

If you choose a colored robe be sure the choice will blend with the colors in the sanctuary. Some churches will take one color but not any other. The lighting should be considered, for a robe which looks well in natural light may take on a peculiar hue when viewed under the artificial lighting of the sanctuary. Personally I feel that it is best to choose one color for all robes for all choirs which sing regularly in the services. There are many churches, however, where a different color is used to distinguish each choir. The danger is that the different colors will not blend with each other or with the church—there is apt to be a hodge-podge of colors reminiscent of an old-fashioned quilt. There is a church in Richmond, Virginia, which chose different colors for the various choirs but matched

121

them skillfully with the colors in the stained glass windows behind the chancel. When the choirs are massed for festivals they seem to be a pleasant continuation of the window behind them.

Whatever your choice of vestment, see that the necklines all fit well and that there is a uniform appearance. I have been in churches where the children came in so disheveled and so dreadful looking that it seemed virtually impossible to get any good music out of the group. Vestments with drooping necklines, with sweaters or dresses showing underneath are not attractive. Lengths must be checked each fall so that the hemlines are even. If the children feel and look right, they are in a better mood to sing right.

This involves work each fall, for children grow tall during the summer and have to be refitted in a new vestment. There is another advantage in having all robes the same color and style—there is less work to do since the different-sized robes can be shifted from one choir to another. The choir mothers should take over this responsibility under the director's guidance. After the robe is fitted, a little tape with the child's name written on it in indelible ink should be sewn in the back of the neck and the robe assigned to a definite place so the child knows which is his robe and where it is to be kept for the year. If there is a choir cap (as is often used with older choirs) it should be kept in the same place and should be labeled with the proper name. Few people like to wear another person's clothing. Also in the younger choirs there are always cases of contagious diseases making the rounds, and there is less likelihood of spreading the germs if each person uses his own vestment.

There is a particular problem which many choir directors have to face. Especially around Christmas time many public schools will ask to borrow your robes for their Christmas concert. While it is good to co-operate wherever possible, so many choir directors have had such unhappy results that in some churches the music committee has made it a rule not to lend vestments unless a child who is a member of the church choir borrows his own with the understanding that the child and his parents are responsible. If the vestments are loaned to a school, this is what often happens: The children are always excited at a Christmas program and when they come back to the rooms they take off their vestments hurriedly (often ripping or tearing the cloth), drop them any place, knock some of them on the floor, where someone else walks on them. Oftentimes the vestments come back badly soiled and have to be cleaned before they can be used again. Even if the school agrees to take care of getting them cleaned, the laundry may be left to the parents and the results are not always uniform or good. There is also the danger that the vestments may not be returned when promised, and the church choir may find itself without them on Sunday morning because they are tightly locked in the school. At best the vestments will be crumpled and mussed and have to be pressed before use.

What about bow ties? The very small child does not mind them, but the older children, especially boys, do not like to wear them. There is an element of "cuteness" about ties which is not helpful in a service of worship, and the long dangling pieces of cloth are a real temptation for pulling. If you feel you must use them, choose some kind that can be pinned, clipped, or fastened securely so there is no danger of their coming untied.

Choir Mothers' Guild

CHAPTER **XIII**

WHO IS GOING TO CARE FOR ALL THESE VEST-
ments? Obviously if you are playing the service
you cannot be at the organ and in the vestries at
the same time. Even if you are only directing you
cannot be with every choir helping each individual.

The answer is a Choir Mothers' Guild, made up of as many
women as you feel you need to help handle the many problems of
a choir program. Most of them will be mothers of choir members,
but the group is not necessarily limited to these. There are many

124

women in the church who would be willing to give time and energy to the Guild and to work through the choir year. The more people you draw into the group, the greater the enthusiasm for the program through the entire church. The Guild can be a wonderful publicity agent for the program, for they will boost it and give it publicity in many ways which would not be open to the director.

During the year you and the chairman of the music committee should be alert to observe people who show an interest in the choir work, and people whose children have been regular in attendance. The minister may also be able to suggest names to you, particularly new members whom you may not have met. Many people offer their services to the minister without any specific job in mind. Grandmothers and elderly persons often have time to help as members of the Guild and are wonderful workers. Ask these persons to serve for the entire year with the understanding that they will not be asked to serve beyond that time unless they wish to continue. The opportunity should be given for a person to drop out if she so desires, but an invitation to stay on should be extended.

It is wise to have a specific group of women assigned to each choir who are responsible for taking care of the vestments, helping with the robing at services, doing telephoning, arranging transportation pools when needed, arranging social gatherings of the choir, helping the smaller children with boots and heavy clothing at rehearsals, and serving in any way which will help the program. It will take a larger group of women for the smaller children since they need more help with vesting. It is also helpful to divide up telephone calling among several people so the burden is not too heavy for anyone. One person should be in charge of telephoning, and she can divide the names and notify the members of the telephone committee when it is necessary to get a message to the children or the parents. The telephone committee is useful through the junior age, but intermediates and above prefer to do their own telephoning and can organize their own calling system.

When the Guild meets for the first time, divide the duties and let each person know what her responsibilities will be for the year. This first meeting can be in the form of a picnic, a coffee hour at the church, or a tea in one of the homes. One year our first meeting was a picnic with box suppers prepared by a restaurant. All the husbands were invited, and the event was held at a nearby farm. After an excellent supper and good fellowship we discussed the calendar of events and divided the responsibilities. It was a fine start for the group.

Our choirs from the junior age up sing every Sunday, so the choir mothers have a real responsibility in getting the children vested and ready for the processional hymn in the short interim between church school and morning worship. They check to see that there are no hair bows, no colored clasps in the hair, and that the children are wearing white socks. A few extra pairs are kept handy! There is also a supply of bobby pins to take care of unruly hair. The mothers stay with the children in the processional line until it begins to move into the church, and one mother sits near the children, not as a monitor but to help in case of illness.

It is best not to have too many mothers around at robing time, for too many cause confusion. Children should be quiet before they enter the church, and the mothers can teach this by word and example. With the small children it is often more effective to have other persons than the children's own parents to help with the vesting. The children are so accustomed to being bombarded with instructions from their parents that they really do not listen to them. If the parents are not members of the Guild they may add to the confusion by giving commands and orders which are contrary to what you have given. It is certainly best to have only a select group in charge and to keep the other parents out of the vestry even though they want to be helpful. If there is a point which all parents and children must pass on the way to the vestry, it may help to station a person there to say to the parents: "I'm sure that Jeannie can go on by herself. She is a big girl now. There are people in the choir room to help, so Jeannie will meet you after church." The mother is not offended and vesting will be smoother. This problem presents itself most often with choirs of very small children who do not sing regularly.

Transportation is often a problem for many families, and the Guild can help greatly at this point. There are many homes where the mother works and is unable to bring her child to choir. Or there may be several children in one family with ages such that several choirs are involved at different hours or different days. Sometimes the father travels and has the car on choir day. If the director is alert, the names of these children can be handed over to the Guild with a request to work out transportation pools. One mother may agree to take a group of children from school to church and home for one month, and then another mother takes over. Sometimes four mothers may agree to take turns—one week a month. Or it may be that a mother can help by keeping a neighbor's child for a short while after rehearsal until the mother returns from work.

One significant contribution that the Guild can make is in arranging choir family nights. Even if the church does have regular family night gatherings, one night could be turned over to the choirs for special emphasis. The date should be determined in consultation with the Guild and the church calendar, avoiding any conflicts with the schools or scouts. The meal can be organized so that each family brings enough food to feed its members plus one. Or the various choirs can be assigned to bring either a meat, a vegetable, a salad, or a dessert. You will find that each church has a procedure which seems to work best, and it is wise to follow that. Milk, coffee, and tea can be provided through the music committee. All the choir members bring their entire families, and dinner is placed on a long table in a central location so everyone has a choice of many different foods. Some churches ask each family to bring their own silver and paper plates, thus eliminating dishwashing and cleanup after the dinner.

Let the choir members wear some special badge, such as musical notes made of construction paper, to indicate their special place of honor, perhaps using a different design or color for each choir. They become the hosts and hostesses for the evening. Encourage the families to sit together as a unit rather than having the various choir groups sit together.

After supper there can be community singing, using song sheets or collections of songs. The leadership for the singing may come from one individual appointed in each choir to lead a certain song. Sometimes the boys' choir can lead, particularly in rounds—which boys enjoy so much. Or it may be one adult who leads the singing.

After a period of singing the age groups can separate, with the children going to another part of the building for games or stories under the supervision of an adult. The older young people may go to another place for folk games or singing. The adults stay in the dining room, and the director has a chance to explain what is happening in the choir program for the year. It is also a time for questions and answers and for discussion of problems which are of concern to parents and director.

The director does need a chance to talk with the parents and to explain the rules and the program. Last year a father, who was new in the church and who had a daughter coming to the junior choir, was surprised at the attendance requirements which had just been explained. "Do you mean to say you expect these children to be here every week and every Sunday morning?" The answer, of course, was yes. He replied, "Well, I think you are being a little too hard on them." When I pointed out that the children, after being in the choir for a while, would see the necessity for being regular in attendance in order to prepare the music well for Sunday morning, he repeated his objection. At this point all of the parents who had children in the choir rose to the defense of the program. The daughter turned out to be one of the most faithful members of the choir, and obviously did not feel imposed upon. The choir dinner really gave a fine opportunity to get across a most important point to many choir parents.

The minister of the church should know of the Choir Mothers' Guild and should be invited to meet with them at some time during the year. He can express appreciation for what they are doing, and at the same time help them understand the value of the choir program and their participation in the ministry of the church through music. He can also point out the importance of their job in keeping the children quiet and orderly so that they are in a proper state of mind for the service of worship.

It is well to express further appreciation to the Guild through a party meeting at least once during the year. It can take place at one of the regular meeting times, but use your best china and serve something rather elaborate for refreshments. Let the Guild know at all times that you think their work is most important and that you are grateful to them for the help they are giving.

Special Services for Children's Choirs

CHAPTER XIV

ONE OF THE BIG SEASONS IN THE CHURCH calendar, especially for children, is the Christmas season. All churches plan musical programs, many of which are called candlelight carol services, and which follow the same general form each year. Sometimes they are called "carols from around the world" and consist of reading a passage of Scripture, singing a carol, reading a passage, singing a carol. This kind of service has been done so much that there is not the enjoyment of it that there should be.

In attempting to keep the season more informal and family centered, we have for many years used a "round the table carol sing." The idea came from Donald Kettring and was first used by him at the Westminster Presbyterian Church in Lincoln, Nebraska. The carol sing is held in the church-school auditorium on a week night, and the choirs are seated at tables. On our small stage we put the kindergarten tables with small chairs, and the younger children sit there. On the floor level we place tables for the other choirs, with the tables radiating out from the stage and with all singers facing the congregation. The piano is placed so I can see and direct all the choirs.

When the choirs come in, it is as if a group of friends were coming together to sing. There is no formal processional. They come in casually and take their places at the tables which are decorated with white tablecloths, green ivy, and red candles. The folders for the music are red and are placed flat on the table in front of each singer.

As the program progresses I talk about the different carols, and the program consists of antiphonal songs, question and answer songs, conversational songs, rounds, and, of course, carols. The congregation is invited to join in singing some of the familiar numbers.

In recent years, as the choirs have increased in number and size, the fire hazard of so many children and lighted candles has caused much anxiety. After one year of having acolytes sitting on the side of the stage to watch for trouble and of having buckets of water and sand placed all around the choirs (concealed, of course) we decided to try something different.

The following year, while we used the same kind of songs, we had most of the choirs sit in groups on the floor level. The boys of boy choir age were dressed in page costumes made of inexpensive colored material by the Choir Mothers. The Junior girls dressed in fancy aprons, and the very small children wore tiny sleigh bells. At the end of the singing the boys came in in procession carrying an enormous fruitcake, flaming on top. We had filled the center hole with sugar, poured vanilla extract over the sugar, and lighted it. This ended the program, and all the children had fruitcake to eat.

Another successful program has been a family carol sing. All the choirs were vested, but instead of sitting as choirs the children sat with their parents and the family unit was emphasized. There was no procession, and there was a feeling of informality. After a few carols were sung by the entire group the minister offered a simple prayer, and then I explained the purpose of the program. I pointed out that some families sang often at home, while perhaps others did not; but at this program everyone was to sing as members of a church family. I told about Martin Luther's idea that the way to teach songs was to teach the children, and they in turn would teach the elders. I said that our choir children had learned many interesting Christmas songs and they wished to share these with, and teach them to, their parents.

The material included fun songs appropriate to Christmas, rounds such as "Christmas Is Coming, the Goose Is Getting Fat," and many fine but unfamiliar carols. From time to time a choir was called to the front to sing a carol which they had especially prepared.

The seven- and eight-year-olds sang the "Waits' Carol" and taught the "Alleluia" refrain to the parents. Then the carol was sung antiphonally between the choir and the parents. They also sang the Polish carol, "Infant Holy" and then invited the parents to try it with them.

The boys sang the carol, "Good Christian Men, Rejoice," using the interpolated measure which is found in some editions of the song. Then later when the parents sang the carol, the boys sang the added measure alone.

In the spiritual "Behold That Star" and in "The Friendly Beasts" we had some of the children sing solo verses—something which cannot be done in the large sanctuary at a worship service.

When the adult choir came forward to sing we used "God Rest Ye Merry" arranged by Henry Pfohl [1] to show how composers of today are putting old carols into modern settings.

The program took just an hour, and it was well received by the choirs and congregation, for we were singing as families just for the fun of singing together. There was plenty of variety and plenty of movement as choirs grouped together, and the adults learned many new numbers.

A variation on the carols of all lands type of program was used by a former student to good advantage. The various choirs learned carols from many nations, and at the December family night program the children dressed in costumes of the different nations. The costumes were made out of inexpensive cloth by the Choir Mothers' Guild. The choir was divided into groups of eight and each group represented a different nationality as they strolled from place to place during the dinner singing their country's carols.

You can build further variation on this theme by using carols with slides to illustrate them. Slides can be purchased or rented from church publishing houses. They can illustrate either the songs themselves or the countries represented. Effective use can also be made of slides of famous paintings of the Christmas message.

When the children have been studying carols of other lands I have tried to find people in the community who have ties with the countries represented. One December we had the German bride of one of our servicemen come to rehearsal and tell the children

[1] New York: Harold Flammer, Incorporated.

about Christmas customs in Germany, then teach them a German song. Another year we had a Chinese student who talked to the children about China, answered questions, and sang a song in Chinese. She wrote the name of each child in Chinese as souvenirs of the afternoon. The children had learned some Chinese songs— in English—and they enjoyed singing these for their visitor.

The Easter season, as well as Christmas, provides opportunity for combining all of the choirs of the church into a great musical expression of joy. Processional anthems of festival nature, antiphonal anthems, additional instrumental accompaniments of brasses and strings, all find a place in the music of these seasons.

Palm Sunday provides an appropriate time for a service which features the children's choirs. In many churches children who have prepared for church membership are received into the church on this Sunday. Why not have these children received into the church at an all-children's service in the afternoon? The chancel may be filled with the young choirs who will assume the whole burden of the musical part of the service. Even the very young choristers may sing the prayer or benediction response and they may join the older children in singing the hymns and a simple introit. Hymns must be carefully selected and only two, or at the most, three stanzas sung. "For the Beauty of the Earth," "Fairest Lord Jesus," "All Things Bright and Beautiful," and similar hymns would be appropriate. The choirs of junior age will have the anthem responsibility and more than one may be used. It is possible to have antiphonal effects between boys and girls, and some anthems may be adjusted so that the younger children may join in on a phrase or two. The entire service should be less than an hour in length and must provide for considerable shifting of position—standing, sitting.

Such a service is eminently suitable for the reception of children into church membership and it gives the choristers a fine experience in leading in worship. With proper preparation the children will not feel that they are on exhibit in concert style, but that they are responsible for smoothness in the mechanics of the service.

America becomes more and more music festival conscious with each passing year, and junior choir festivals are a part of the annual music program in many communities. Such festivals, if well planned and executed, make a vital contribution to the life of the child and to his church. Every church that encourages its choirs to participate in festivals is indicating the breadth of its thinking and its willingness to be ecumenical minded.

Many small churches have comparably few children in their choir groups and for these a festival provides opportunity for the stimulation that singing in a large group affords. Even choirs from larger churches may not have many other opportunities for this enlarged experience.

Festival participation, particularly if the festival is held near the end of the choir year, will give choirs a long-range goal toward which to work. After an Easter which has come early in the spring there is often a noticeable let down for the rest of the season unless some such challenging program is ahead. Since there is no room for dead wood in a festival chorus, the requirement of learning all of the music has been known to keep many a laggard alert.

Festivals can, however, be just as valueless as valuable unless they are carefully planned and unless the individual director meets the opportunity with enthusiasm. It is easy to understand why some directors look upon these events with cautious reserve when we see the unorganized efforts of some planning committees. Much detail work should be done months ahead of the festival date, in fact, a whole year ahead is not too soon to begin preparations. Music

135

must be selected, a festival director chosen and arrangements made for a suitable location for the festival. If several denominations are represented in a festival, the music selection committee should include one from each denomination so that festival music may be used throughout the year in individual churches with no doctrinal offense to anyone. To hoard anthems for festival use only seems impractical and foolish. But, if chosen anthems are to be used throughout the year they must be in the hands of the directors as they begin their fall choir routines. Any young choir sings best when the music is memorized and certainly no festival chorus of children has ever sung well when its attention was divided between music scores and director. This necessitates a long period of preparation.

If a festival is to be a community project, choirs of all churches must be invited to participate. A letter to each director gives information about the over-all plan and invites him to be present at a meeting of all directors. At that meeting a chairman must be selected so that meetings will move on a businesslike basis. A secretary and a treasurer also need to be elected.

In many cities each participating church pays a fee to help defray expenses and this, plus the offering taken, generally assures a self-supporting festival. Expenses include printed programs, publicity, advertising, and sexton's fee. A local director contributes his services but one brought from a distance must be paid. Each choir director handles the publicity in his own church and the general chairman appoints a general publicity chairman who is responsible for city wide coverage in newspapers and on radio.

Because most festivals are designed on a worship pattern the logical place for holding them is in a church. Chancels are never large enough to hold several hundred children who must spill out into the nave. The church which lends itself to the most satisfactory arrangement for singers and director must therefore be chosen. There must also be room for the processional to move with dignity. An impressive ending for the processional is the appearance of the ministers and choir directors of each church represented, the corresponding minister and director walking together, each vested. This group sits in a specially reserved place near the choirs. Ministers of various denominations will offer prayers, read the Scriptures, and preside at the taking of the offering.

There are good reasons for employing an out of town director for the festival, but there are just as many good reasons for using a local director. Perhaps a good plan is to rotate between these two possibilities. If an out of town director is to work efficiently he must be a member of the music selection group. Actually, all of the directors of participating choirs are ex officio members of this committee and should not only feel free to suggest anthems, but should be encouraged to do so. Festival music should not be so difficult as to eliminate the choirs of small churches nor should it be music which requires a choir of sizable proportions in order to sound well. Unison anthems are generally preferable for junior age choirs, but they need the variety of occasional descants and canon style treatment. Hymns should be a part of the program, also, and they too should be memorized, with caution being taken to see that all choirs learn exactly the same text. The entire program need not be over forty-five minutes in length, in fact it is well to err on the side of brevity!

Final rehearsals may move smoothly and rapidly toward the climax of a fine festival or they may be a period of utter chaos and confusion, depending again upon advance preparation. An individual or a committee should have the responsibility of seating the choirs and instructing them in processional and recessional procedure. Choir seating calls for attention to heights of children and colors of vestments so as to produce a chorus that is as appealing to the eye as to the ear. Diagrams of the seating arrangements given to each director ahead of time with instructions to have her own group ready to take its festival place quickly will save at least an hour of precious rehearsal time. These diagrams will indicate which rows each choir is to occupy and the number of children to sit in each row. If the taller children are to occupy the outside seats this should be noted, thus the actual seating line-up may be prepared in individual rehearsals and it will then need nothing more than putting together at festival time. Directors usually need reminding about making a double check on choristers in order that no colored hair bows or fancy hair clips are worn with vestments and to make sure that there is no chewing gum under the tongue.

Processionals and recessionals may be and should be dignified and beautiful. There must be no last minute flurry of preparation and this requires a sufficient number of marshals to quietly and easily assemble the final line-up. Then, after a prayer, the group moves into a wonderful musical and spiritual experience.

Choirs and the Church School

XV

STRANGELY ENOUGH, IT HAS ONLY BEEN COMPAR-
atively recently that we have begun to realize that
children's choirs belong to the church school as
well as to the church. And what expanded oppor-
tunities are afforded the choirs and the church-school departments if
they correlate and co-ordinate! Both groups recognize the fact that
much factual teaching is done through singing, yet the brief time
allotted to the church school and/or the timidity of many teachers in
trying to teach songs often restricts the use of music in department

classes. Then again, if music is used, it is too often used solely as an end in itself and not as a teaching aid also. When this is the case, the same songs are sung Sunday after Sunday in endless repetition.

The advantages in co-operative work need hardly be mentioned. The church-school teacher will have the benefit of professional help in the teaching of song materials suggested in church-school materials, as well as having further music material suggested by the choir director. This enables the teacher to make use of more music and a wider variety of music with less time necessary for teaching music in the classes. We would not suggest, however, that all music teaching be delegated to the choir, for learning songs should be a part of the church-school class experience.

The choir director, through her study of lesson helps for the various department teachers, is constantly adding valuable song material to her library. She is also adding to her own knowledge of what her denomination feels is suitable teaching material for each age level.

Each director should ask for a set of the teaching materials for each department of the church school which has a related choir. She needs to know what units are being studied, what the goals are, what song material is suggested, and what poster material will be used. The suggested music must then be carefully studied and evaluated, both text-wise and music-wise. She can select and begin work on other music which will be related to the lesson theme—hymns, anthems, and responses.

The director will certainly have many hymnals and song collections beyond those owned by the department and from which additional materials may be selected for augmenting the teaching unit. *Songs from Luke* and *Songs from Matthew*, both with music by Lee H. Bristol, Jr., and texts by David Demarest, are unusual and serviceable. Beside the director's edition there is an attractive junior edition which presents, along with nicely illustrated song material, information about the part of the Bible from which the song originates.

Our Songs of Praise has in its indexes a list of hymns correlated with Bible stories from both Old and New Testaments. This book also has a good index of hymns suitable for the various seasons of the church year.

We Go to Church has many excellent songs that contribute to the educational processes of young Christians. The index lists them as praise, prayer, service, and learning songs. Each song is attractively illustrated.

Director and teacher will undoubtedly need planning sessions together in preparing a new unit. Each must know what and how the other is planning to present his part of the program, and music teaching duties must be properly divided. The director can give further help by showing teachers how to teach a song.

At a teachers' meeting or a training session the director could teach the song material in the next unit lessons to the teachers—showing how they in turn can teach the songs to the children most effectively. Teachers need to gain confidence in singing without a piano, for many classrooms have no such instrument and even if one is provided, much is lost while the teacher goes to the piano, sounds the pitch, and then starts. These informal gatherings of teachers are just the place to learn to sing easily and confidently. Many people are embarrassed to admit that they do not know how to handle music well, and sometimes the director is reticent in offering her services for fear her motives will be misunderstood. Likewise some teachers feel that they have no right to ask for help from the choir director—she is too busy with choirs and the morning worship service and would not have the time or even be interested in trying to help the church school with its music problems.

Director and teacher must come together to share in the important job of Christian education through all the means possible. Training schools for Christian educators should include courses in church music planned at the level of need for every teacher. Too many teachers who need the help stay away because, as they say, "I don't know anything about music." It is precisely these teachers who need to come, and the choir director must be willing and able to offer help.

Choir directors should also be concerned about training pianists for the church school, for no church ever has enough. To solve the problem we must work steadily at encouraging our young people to learn to play hymns, and the local piano teacher to teach hymn playing. Perhaps some piano teachers avoid this field for the very reason that hymn playing is difficult, but probably most spend little time on hymns because they are more interested in preparing their students to play recital pieces publicly. When I have talked about this problem to piano teachers, they expressed a willingness to undertake teaching hymn playing but had just not felt any need or pressure for it. There were some few children who wanted to learn to play hymns, but the majority had given no thought to it.

In Burlington, North Carolina, the piano teachers association has become so interested in the problem that they have sponsored for several years a hymn playing contest among the students of the city. Every child is encouraged to learn the prescribed hymns—the smaller children use simplified versions—and as many as sixty players have competed in a single year. This is one city where the supply of good pianists is not apt to be a problem!

Much harm can be done in the children's departments if the piano is not well played, and sometimes it is better to use no piano at all. The finest adult players should be used with the smallest children. At the junior age and above we should encourage the children who are able to play well to do some of the accompanying of the hymns. The choice of hymns in advance is a must if youngsters are to play accurately and effectively. It takes practice to be able to play a hymn, but even more practice to play a hymn to lead people in singing. The director can encourage the children in the choir to play hymns for her and when they can handle a particular hymn this information can be relayed to the department leader. Additional experience can be gained at informal meetings such as a choir family night supper, when the singing is apt to go well in spite of the pianist. This manner of working the children into the program of the church without the competition angle is perhaps better than learning a hymn for a contest and never playing it anywhere else.

All of this involves time, thought, and hard work, and it is much easier to sit back and criticize the music in the church school. But if we are really ministers of music our ministry must extend far beyond the choir. It does not stop with the Sunday worship services —it extends into the whole church school and into every corner of the life of the church.

Appendix

MATERIALS FOR PRIMARY CHOIRS

Song Material

Grime, William. *New Carols and Songs for Children*. New York: Carl Fischer, Incorporated, 1949.

Hymns for Primary Worship. Philadelphia: Westminster Press, 1946.

Klammer, Edward, ed. *Our Songs of Praise*. St. Louis, Missouri: Concordia Publishing House, 1955.

Landeck, Beatrice. *Songs to Grow On*. New York: Edward Marks Music Corporation, 1950.

Marshall, Jane, and Montgomery, Mary Elizabeth. *We Go to Church*. New York: Carl Fischer, Incorporated, 1956.

Mason, Anges Leckie, and Ohanian, Phyllis Brown. *God's Wonderful World*. New York: New American Library of World Literature, Incorporated, 1954.

Pooler, Marie. *A Child Sings*. Minneapolis: Augsburg Publishing House, 1958.

Thomas, Edith Lovell. *Sing, Children, Sing*. Nashville: Abingdon-Cokesbury Press, 1939.

Thomas, Edith Lovell. *The Whole World Singing*. New York: Friendship Press, 1950.

Songs for Early Childhood. Philadelphia: Westminster Press, 1958.

MATERIALS FOR THE JUNIOR CHOIR

Anthem Collections

"Anthems for the Junior Choir," Books I, II, and III. Philadelphia: Westminster Press, 1944, 1950, and 1954.

Bristol, Lee H., Jr. *Songs from Luke*. East Orange, New Jersey: Canyon Press, 1953.

Bristol, Lee H., Jr. *Songs from Matthew*. East Orange, New Jersey: Canyon Press, 1957.

Davis, Katherine K., ed. *The Belfry Book*. New York: Gamble Hinged Music Company, 1943.

Davis, Katherine K., ed. *Green Hill Junior Choir Book*. Boston: E. C. Schirmer Music Company, 1938.

Holler, John. "Junior Choir Anthem Book." Books II and V. New York: H. W. Gray Company.

Lenel, Ludwig. *Songs for Children's Voices*. Fremont, Ohio: Chantry Music Press, 1949.

Willan, Healey. *We Praise Thee*. St. Louis, Missouri: Concordia Publishing House.

Williams, David H. *Junior Choir Anthems*. Evanston, Illinois: Summy-Birchard Publishing Company, 1953.

Anthems

Bach; Come, Let Us All This Day; E. C. Schirmer.
Bach; Come, Together Let Us Sing; E. C. Schirmer.
Bach; My Heart Ever Faithful; E. C. Schirmer.
Button; Jesu, Whom Thy Children Love; Gray.
Davies; All Things Bright and Beautiful; Novello.
Davies; May the Grace of Christ; Novello.
Davis, arr.; Let All Things Now Living; E. C. Schirmer.
Dickinson; List to the Lark; Gray.
Gillette; Be Thou My Vision; Kjos.
Grieg-Black; Jesus, Blest Redeemer; Gray.
Hokanson; Good Shepherd of the Children; Kjos.
Holler; Our Shepherd; Gray.
Jacob, arr.; Brother James' Air; Oxford University Press.
Kettring; God Watches Over All the World; Gray.
Kindermann; Dear Christians, Praise God Evermore; Concordia.
Lenel; All Praise to Thee, Eternal God; Concordia.
Lovelace; Kindly Spring Again Is Here; J. Fischer.
Rathbone; The Children's Song; Novello.
Rawls; Touch Hands Around the Rolling World; J. Fischer.
Sharman; A Spring Prayer; Ed. Arnold and Company.

Warner; Let Us With a Gladsome Mind; Summy-Birchard.
White; A Prayer of St. Richard of Chichester; Oxford University Press.
Willan; Come, Jesus, Holy Child; Concordia.
Williams; Give Thanks; Flammer.
York; For the Beauty of the Earth; C. Fischer.

Christmas Anthems

Baker; Whence Is That Goodly Fragrance; Summy-Birchard.
Brook; Silver Lamps; Oxford University Press.
Catalon Carol; Gifts for the Christ Child; Tracy Music Library.
Holler; The Little Jesus; Gray.
Kohler; A Thousand Christmas Candles Now; Novello.
Kountz; Rise Up Early; Galaxy.
Lovelace; Peace On Earth; Choral Services, Incorporated.
Milford; In the Bleak Midwinter; C. Fischer.
Ohanian; The Shepherd Boy; Flammer.
Shaw; The Animals Carol; Novello.
Tatton; The Christ Child; Summy-Birchard.
Wiant; A Chinese Christmas Carol; Gray.
Willan; Bethl'em Lay a-Sleeping; Concordia.
Willan; Two Christmas Carols; Frederick Harris Company.
Williams, arr.; On Christmas Night; Galaxy.
Williams; To Bethlehem; Gray.

Lent and Easter Anthems

Bach-Whitford; Now Winter Fades From Sight; J. Fischer.
Bitgood; Christ the Lord Is Born; Galaxy.
Davies; Easter Bell Carol; Flammer.
Eichhorn; Song for Easter; Gray.
Hill; The Whole Bright World Rejoices; Gray.
Holler; An Easter Carol; Gray.
Lovelace; Easter Flowers Are Blooming Bright; Gray.
Lovelace; The World Itself Keeps Easter Day; Choral Services, Incorporated.
Marryott; One Early Easter Morning; Gray.

MATERIALS FOR THE JUNIOR HIGH CHOIR

Anthem Collections

"Anthems for the Youth Choir." Book I. Philadelphia: Westminster Press, 1952.

Davis, Katherine K., ed. *Green Hill Junior Choir Book*. Boston: E. C. Schirmer Music Company, 1938.

Davis, Katherine K., ed. *Green Hill Three Part Book*. Boston: E. C. Schirmer Music Company, 1930.

Hokanson, Margarethe, and Michelson, Thelma. *Alleluia*. Chicago: Neil A Kjos Music Company, 1955.

Holler, John. "Junior Choir Anthem Book." Books I, III, and IV. New York: H. W. Gray Company.

Ringwald, Roy. *Praise Him*. Delaware Water Gap, Pennsylvania: Shawnee Press.

Thomas, Paul. *The Morning Star Choir Book*. St. Louis, Missouri: Concordia Publishing House.

The Treble Choir. Minneapolis: Schmitt, Hall, and McCreary Company, 1943.

Willan, Healey. *We Praise Thee*. St. Louis, Missouri: Concordia Publishing House, 1953.

Anthems

Akerman; Jesu, Joyance of My Heart; Novello.
Attwood; Songs of Praise the Angels Sang; Novello.
Bach; At Thy Feet; B. F. Wood.
Bach-Harts; Lord God, We Worship Thee; Summy-Birchard.
Borowski; Angels of Light; FitzSimons.
Bortniansky-Black; O God of Might; Gray.
Brackett-Larson; Jesus, Our Good Shepherd; Summy-Birchard.
Brook; The Shepherd; Oxford University Press.
Caldwell; Spring Prayer; Birchard.
Clokey; Jehovah's Throne; Flammer.
Clokey, arr.; Litany of Jesus; Flammer.
Clokey; Our Master Hath a Garden; Summy-Birchard.
Darst; O God of Youth; Gray.
Davies; Had We But Hearkened; Novello.
Davis; Our God Is a Rock; Summy-Birchard.

Dvořák; I Will Sing Thee Songs of Gladness; G. Schirmer.
Handel; O Lovely Peace ("Judas Maccabaeus"); Gray.
Jones; Little Lamb, Who Made Thee; C. Fischer.
Larson; Come, Children, Join to Sing; Schmitt.
Larson; O Christ, the Way; Schmitt.
Larson, arr.; Walk in the Light; Summy-Birchard.
Lenel; All Praise to God Who Reigns Above; Concordia.
Lenel; Lord, This Day Thy Children Meet; Concordia.
Lutkin; Above the Clear Blue Sky; FitzSimons.
Marcello; And With Songs I Will Celebrate; Concordia.
Marcello; Give Ear Unto Me; Gray.
Pfautsch; I Lift My Eyes; Summy-Birchard.
Pfautsch; The Ten Commandments; Summy-Birchard.
Pfautsch; What the Lord Requires; Summy-Birchard.
Shure; His Beauty Now Appears; Belwin.
Thiman; A Seasonal Thanksgiving; G. Shirmer.
Turner-Harts; O Clap Your Hands Together; Summy-Birchard.
Whittlesey; We Tread Upon Thy Carpets; Flammer.
Wienhorst; Choral Settings for The Seasons; Concordia.
Wienhorst; Come, Ye Children, Praise the Savior; Concordia.
Willan; Holy Spirit, Hear Us; Concordia.

Christmas Anthems

Couper, arr.; Here With the Ox and Donkey Gray; J. Fischer.
Couper, arr.; The Flute Carol; J. Fischer.
Barnard; Let Our Gladness Know No End; Summy-Birchard.
Darst; All My Heart This Night Rejoices; Gray.
Davis, arr.; Mary's Lullaby; Summy-Birchard.
Davis; To the Manger; Summy-Birchard.
Dickinson, arr.; O Nightingale, Awake; Gray.
Dickinson, arr.; Sleep, My Jesus, Sleep; Gray.
Eldridge; Torches; Novello.
Franck; At the Cradle; E. C. Schirmer.
Clokey; Good Friends, Give Ear and Sing Noel; Summy-Birchard.
Hokanson; A Joyous Christmas Song; Summy-Birchard.
Johnson; Carol of the Singing Reeds; J. Fischer.
Kountz; Carol of the Sheep Bells; Galaxy.

Luvaas; Alleluia, Christ Is Born; Summy-Birchard.
Praetorius; Rejoice, Ye Christian Men, Rejoice; E. C. Schirmer.
Reger; The Virgin's Slumber Song; Associated Music Publishers.
Reinecke; A Christmas Carol; Gray.
Shimmin, arr.; In Bethlehem; C. Fischer.
Traditional; The Coventry Carol; Novello.
Willan; The Story of Bethlehem (Christmas Cantata).; Concordia.
Willan; When the Herds Were Watching; Concordia.

Lent and Easter

Bach-Buzzin; Christ Is Arisen from the Grave; Concordia.
Bach; Up, Up! My Heart, With Gladness; E. C. Schirmer.
Clokey; Welcome Happy Morning; Flammer.
Davis, arr.; Awake, Thou Wintry Earth; E. C. Schirmer.
Dickinson, arr.; In Joseph's Lovely Garden; Gray.
Dickinson, arr.; This Glad Easter Day; Gray.
Garden, arr.; Easter Carol; Gray.
Thompson; Spring Bursts Today; Gray.
Tschaikowsky; Legend; Gray.
Willan; Hosanna to the Son of David; Concordia.

ANTHEMS FOR COMBINED CHOIRS

Bach-Dickinson; O Saviour Sweet; Gray.
Bach-Dickinson; In Faith I Calmly Rest; Gray.
Dickinson; List to the Lark; Gray.
Holst; A Festival Chime; Galaxy.
Lapo; This Is My Father's World; R. D. Row.
Larson; To God All Praise and Glory; Summy-Birchard.
Lockwood; All Thy Works Praise Thee; Gray.
Malin, arr.; Praise the Lord, Ye Heavens Adore Him; Summy-Birchard.
Olds, arr.; St. Francis' Hymn; Schmitt, Hall, and McCreary.
Reimann-Dickinson; Dearest Jesus, Gentle, Mild; Gray.
Schneider, arr.; Children of the Heavenly Father; Flammer.
Thiman; A Seasonal Thanksgiving; G. Schirmer.

ANTHEMS FOR CHRISTMAS
(COMBINED CHOIRS)

Bach-Buzzin; Now Sing We, Now Rejoice; Concordia.
Davis; As It Fell Upon a Night; Galaxy.
Dickinson; The Citizens of Chatres; Gray.
Holst, arr.; Christmas Song; G. Schirmer.
Jungst, arr.; While By Our Sleeping Flocks We Lay; E. C. Schirmer.
Lockwood; Lightly, Lightly, Bells Are Pealing; Gray.
Lovelace; From Eastern Lands; Summy-Birchard.
Niles, arr.; When Jesus Lived in Galilee; G. Schirmer.
Purvis, arr.; What Strangers Are These; Summy-Birchard.
Spilman-Bingham; Away in a Manger; Gray.

ANTHEMS FOR LENT AND EASTER
(COMBINED CHOIRS)

Bitgood; Hosanna; Gray.
Davis; Alleluia, Come, Good People; Galaxy.
Hill; The Whole Bright World Rejoices; Gray.
Holler; The Risen Christ; Gray.
Marryott; One Early Easter Morning; Ditson.
Marryott, arr.; We Will Be Merry; Gray.
Vulpius; Praise to Our God; Boston Music Company.

HYMNALS AND SONGBOOKS

Alexander, C. M., ed. *At Worship*. New York: Harper and Bros., 1951.
The Beacon Song and Service Book. Boston: Beacon Press, 1935.
Bristol, Lee H., Jr. *Thirty-five Sacred Rounds and Canons*. East Orange, New Jersey: Canyon Press, 1955.
Bristol, Lee H., Jr., and Friedell, Harold W. *Hymns for Children and Grownups*. New York: Farrar, Straus, and Cudahy, Incorporated, 1953.

The Canyon Hymnal for Boys and Girls. East Orange, New Jersey: Canyon Press, 1958.

The Children's Hymnal. St. Louis, Missouri: Concordia Publishing House, 1955.

Cooper, Irving. *The Singing Teens.* Niagara Falls, New York: Gordon V. Thompson, Limited,

Cooper, Irving. *Tune Time for Teen Time.* New York: Carl Fischer, Incorporated.

Dearmer, G., Williams, R. V., and Shaw, M., eds. *The Oxford Book of Carols.* London: Oxford University Press, 1928.

Hymns for Junior Worship. Philadelphia: Westminster Press, 1940.

Hymns for Primary Worship. Philadelphia: Westminster Press, 1946.

Kettring, Donald D. *Familiar Hymns With Descants.* Philadelphia: Westminster Press, 1936.

Klammer, Edward. *Our Songs of Praise.* St. Louis, Missouri: Concordia Publishing House, 1955.

Smith, H. Augustine. *The New Hymnal for American Youth.* Westwood, New Jersey: Fleming H. Revell Company.

Thomas, Edith Lovell. *Singing Worship.* Nashville: Abingdon Press, 1935.

Wilson, Harry Robert. *Rounds and Canons.* Minneapolis: Schmitt, Hall, and McCreary Company, 1943.

Bibliography

CHOIR ORGANIZATION AND CHILDREN'S CHOIRS

Davison, Archibald Thompson. *Church Music—Illusion and Reality*. Cambridge, Massachusetts: Harvard University Press, 1952.

Jacobs, Ruth Krehbiel. *The Children's Choir*. Rock Island, Illinois: Augustana Press, 1958.

Jacobs, Ruth Krehbiel. *The Successful Children's Choir*. Chicago: H. T. Fitz-Simons Company.

Kettring, Donald. *Steps Toward a Singing Church*. Philadelphia: Westminster Press, 1948.

Vosseller, Elizabeth Van Fleet. *The Use of a Children's Choir in the Church*. New York: H. W. Gray Company, 1907.

Whittlesey, Federal Lee. *A Comprehensive Program of Church Music*. Philadelphia: Westminster Press, 1957.

BOOKS ABOUT HYMNS

Bailey, Albert E. *The Gospel in Hymns*. New York: Charles Scribner's Sons, 1951.

Haeussler, Armin. *The Story of Our Hymns*. St. Louis, Missouri: Eden Publishing House, 1952.

Herzel, Catherine and Frank. *To Thee We Sing*. Philadelphia: Muhlenberg Press.

The Hymnal. 1940 Companion. New York: The Church Pension Fund, 1949.

McCutchen, Robert Guy. *Our Hymnody*. Nashville: Abingdon-Cokesbury Press, 1937.

WORSHIP AND THE ARTS

Bailey, Albert E. *The Arts and Religion.* New York: The Macmillan Company, 1944.

Bainton, Roland. *The Church of Our Fathers.* New York: Charles Scribner's Sons, 1941.

Fitch, Florence Mary. *One God, the Ways We Worship Him.* New York: Lothrop, Lee, and Shepard Company, 1944.

Fitch, Florence Mary. *Their Search for God.* New York: Lothrop, Lee, and Shepard Company, 1947.

Gibson, George M. *The Story of the Christian Year.* Nashville: Abingdon-Cokesbury Press, 1945.

Lillie, Amy Morris. *I Will Build My Church.* Philadelphia: Westminster Press, 1950.

McGee, Ratha D. *Symbols, Signposts of Devotion.* Nashville: The Upper Room, 1956.

McIlwain, Orene. *Worship God.* Richmond, Virginia: John Knox Press, 1954.

Murray, Joseph J. *Children's Story Sermons for Today.* Richmond, Virginia: John Knox Press, 1946.

Smith, Jean Louise. *Great Art and Children's Worship.* Nashville: Abingdon Press, 1948.

Stafford, Thomas A. *Christian Symbolism in the Evangelical Churches.* Nashville: Abingdon Press, 1942.

Wilson, Frank E. *An Outline of Christian Symbolism.* New York: Morehouse-Gorham Company, 1938.

VOCAL TRAINING AND TEACHING MUSIC

Boyter, Mabel Stewart. *My Musical Game Book.* New York: Carl Fischer, Incorporated.

Boyter, Mabel Stewart. *My Musical Puzzle Book.* New York: Carl Fischer, Incorporated.

Boyter, Mabel Stewart. *My Look and Listen Book.* New York: Carl Fischer, Incorporated.

Carabo-Cone, Madeline, and Royt, Beatrice. *How to Help Children Learn Music.* New York: Harper and Bros., 1955.

Landeck, Beatrice. *Children and Music*. New York: William Sloane Associates, 1952.

McKenzie, Duncan. *Training the Boy's Changing Voice*. New Brunswick, New Jersey: Rutgers University Press, 1956.

Marshall, Madeline. *The Singer's Manual of English Diction*. New York: G. Schirmer, Incorporated, 1953.

Myers, Louise K. *Teaching Children Music in the Elementary School*. 2nd ed. Englewood Cliffs, New Jersey: Prentice-Hall, Incorporated, 1956.

Nordholm, Harriet, and Thompson, C. S. *Keys to Teaching Elementary School Music*. Minneapolis: Paul A. Schmitt Music Company, 1949.

Nye, Robert E. and Vernice T. *Music in the Elementary School*. Englewood Cliffs, New Jersey: Prentice-Hall, Incorporated, 1957.

Sheehy, Emma Dickson. *There's Music in Children*. New York: Henry Holt and Company, 1952.

Von Hesse, Elisabeth. *So to Speak*. Philadelphia: J. B. Lippincott Company, 1941.

MUSIC IN CHRISTIAN EDUCATION

Morsch, Vivian Sharp. *The Use of Music in Christian Education*. Philadelphia: Westminster Press, 1956.

Shields, Elizabeth. *Music in the Religious Growth of Children*. Nashville: Abingdon Press, 1943.

Thomas, Edith Lovell. *Music in Christian Education*. Nashville: Abingdon Press, 1953.

CHILD PSYCHOLOGY

Hurlock, Elizabeth B. *Child Development*. New York: McGraw-Hill Publishing Company, 1956.

Jersild, Arthur T. *Child Psychology*. New York: Prentiss-Hall Incorporated, 1947.

Merry, Frieda and R. V. *The First Decades of Life*. New York: Harper and Brothers, 1950.

Strang, Ruth. *Introduction to Child Study*. New York: The Macmillan Company, 1951.

RHYTHMS FOR CHILDREN

Andrews, Gladys. *Creative Rhythmic Movement for Children.* Englewood Cliffs, New Jersey: Prentice-Hall, Incorporated, 1954.

Driver, Ann. *Music and Movement.* New York: Oxford University Press, 1936.

Eele, Marjorie, and Davies, Leila. *Carols for Acting.* London: Novello and Company, 1951.

Fisk, Margaret Palmer. *The Art of the Rhythmic Choir.* New York: Harper and Bros., 1950.

Geri, Frank H. *Illustrated Games and Rhythms for Children.* Englewood Cliffs, New Jersey: Prentice-Hall, Incorporated, 1955.

Millen, Nina. *Children's Games from Many Lands.* New York: Friendship Press, 1951.

SERVICE ORGANIZATIONS

Association for Childhood Education International, Washington, D. C.
 Children and Music.
 Music for Children's Living.
 Songs Children Like.
Cooperative Recreation Service, Delaware, Ohio.
 The Handy Songbook.
 Sing a Tune.

Index